HARRY REID was born in Glasgow and educated in Aberdeen, Edinburgh and Oxford. He trained to be a journalist in Newcastle and then worked in the Scottish Press for 33 years, mainly on the *Scotsman* and the *Herald*, of which he was Editor. In 2001 he was awarded honorary doctorates by Edinburgh and Glasgow Universities for his services to Scottish journalism. He is a former chairman of the Scottish Editors' Committee. He has written a bestselling study of the Church of Scotland and three other books. He is currently working on a commissioned history of the European Reformation. His wife is the travel writer Julie Davidson.

PAUL HENDERSON SCOTT was born in Edinburgh and educated at the Royal High School and Edinburgh University. He was in 52nd (Lowland) and 7th Armed Divisions during the war and then joined the Diplomatic Service. He was in Berlin during the whole of the Soviet blockade and in Cuba during the Missile Crisis. In 1980 he returned to Edinburgh. Since then he has been Rector of Dundee University, President of both the Saltire Society and Scottish PEN, and Vice-President of the SNP and its Spokesman on Culture and International Affairs as well as writing more than a dozen books and editing another dozen or so. His books include: *Walter Scott and Scotland*, *John Galt*, *Towards Independence*, *Andrew Fletcher and the Treaty of Union*, *Still in Bed with an Elephant*, *Defoe in Edinburgh and Other Papers*, *The Boasted Advantages*, *A 20th Century Life* (his autobiography), *Scotland Resurgent*, *The Union of 1707: Why and How*, *The Age of Liberation* and *The New Scotland*.

NEIL KAY has Bachelors and Doctorate degrees from Stirling and is Professor (Emeritus) Economics Dept., University of Strathclyde; Special Professor in the Business School, University of Nottingham; and was Visiting Professor Economics Department, University of Queensland, Australia, 2005, 2006 and 2007. He has also held two Visiting Associate Professorships in the University of California and a part-time Professorship in the Economics Department in the EC's official university in Florence. He is author of six books and numerous articles on industrial economics and the economics of corporate strategies. He lives in Cowal, Argyll with his wife Lorna and two children, Katerina and Kieran.

After serving time on the hulk of HMS Britain, TOM NAIRN escaped to teaching 'Nationalism Studies' at Edinburgh University, then to researching 'Globalisation and Nationalism' at the Royal Melbourne Institute of Technology in Victoria, Australia. His book *The Break-up of Britain* appeared in 1977 (Verso Books, most recent edition Common Ground Publishing, Melbourne, 2003). *Faces of Nationalism* (Verso) appeared in 1997 and *Global Matrix* (Pluto Press, with Paul James) in 2005.

BETTY DAVIES was described in 1989 by Liz Smith Fashion Editor of the *Times* as 'An unexpected visionary in the field of fashion'. Fashion, business and the arts have shaped her career. The launch of the innovative Campus shops in five university cities brought leading fashion designers to a discriminating market of professional women for over 25 years. Her stylish classic designs often in unique and colourful Harris Tweed established her as Scotland's most influential designer. In 1993, she set up Scottish Fashion International, a corporate wear company, with her partner Douglas Henderson. By the end of the '90s SFI was managing over £5m of garment production a year in Scotland and the UK. Betty Davies' branding of Scotland's two major banks gave them instant recognition. Her Royal Blue Watch tartan design for the Royal Bank is evident in every branch in the UK. Her designs for ceremonial dress add colour to many of Scotland's leading formal, academic and royal occasions, a craft she continues to practise. Betty Davies has led an active public life in England and Scotland. She was instrumental in initiating the Edinburgh Theatre Workshop and was its Founder Chairman. She has served on the Press Council, as a magistrate, and as a Member of Court of Nottingham University. She has served as a Governor of the Edinburgh College of Art and was made an Honorary Fellow in 2004 for her contribution to arts education and the visual and performing arts. She presently works as a consultant in the fields of art and communication. During her lifetime Betty Davies has remained mute on her political allegiance. She considers her contribution to *The Independence Book* as her first and only foray in the political arena. It is prompted as a tribute to the life and work of the late Douglas Henderson.

Viewpoints is an occasional series exploring issues of current and future relevance.

Luath Press is an independently owned and managed book publishing company based in Scotland, and is not aligned to any political party or grouping.

The Independence Book

Scotland in today's world

Edited by

HARRY REID and PAUL HENDERSON SCOTT

with contributions by the Editors and

BETTY DAVIES, NEIL KAY and TOM NAIRN

Luath Press Limited

EDINBURGH

www.luath.co.uk

First published 2008
Reprinted 2008

ISBN (10): 1-906307-90-3
ISBN (13): 978-1-906307-90-5

The paper used in this book is recyclable. It is made from low chlorine pulps produced in a low energy, low emission manner from renewable forests.

Printed and bound by
Bell & Bain Ltd., Glasgow

Typeset in 11 point Sabon by
3btype.com

Contents

Reekie, 2000 7

Introduction 9

CHAPTER 1 Make a Noble Dream Come True 11
HARRY REID

CHAPTER 2 Independence is the Answer 29
PAUL HENDERSON SCOTT

CHAPTER 3 The Fish, The Ferry, and The Black Crude Reality 53
NEIL KAY

CHAPTER 4 Scotland and Globalisation 76
TOM NAIRN

CHAPTER 5 An English Voice in Scotland 91
BETTY DAVIES

Postscript PAUL HENDERSON SCOTT, NEIL KAY and BETTY DAVIES 101

Reekie, 2000

Paul Henderson Scott

For Dunbar it was the mirry toun.
Fergusson cried it a canty hole
And like a keek o glore and heaven forby
Here Hume transformed human thocht
And gave bien denners tae his freens.
Clerk Maxwell as a bairn at schule
Scrievit a paper for the Royal Society.

For thae that hae the lugs tae hear
Thae splores, high jinks, high thochts
Sill echo roon closes, wynds,
Howfs and new toun drawing rooms.
In oor ain time Garioch and Smith
Were guy sib to Fergusson himsel.
The sheer beauty o the place still lifts the hert,
A beauty which some hae done their best tae hash

For there's muckle to gar ye grue
In Auld Reikie and in aw Scotland thae days:
Puirtith, ignorance and hopelessness,
Shoddy bigins, ill health, early daith,
Amang the warst in Europe tae oor shame.
Cheek by jowl wi commercial greed,
Affluence, mobile phones and jaunts tae Bangkok,
Efter three hunner year o nae government or misgovernment.

But noo there's a glisk o hope.
At last we hae oor Parliament back,
Reined yet by Westminster,
But sune we'll ding thae traces doon.
Ower lang oor caws for equality and social justice
Hae fallen on deif and distant lugs.
Sune we shall bigg a new and fairer Scotland
Wi Reikie a real capital aince mair.

Introduction

THE AUTHORS, four men and one woman, of the five essays in this book are not exactly in the first flush of youth. Indeed they have a collective age of over 300. They are respected figures who have achieved considerable success in their own fields. They also have wide experience of what is known as 'the real world'. Each of them feels young in spirit, not least because of their enthusiasm for Scottish independence.

Their voices are individual and distinctive, and their perspectives are very different. But they are bound together by one essential denominator – their total commitment to the imperative of independence. That is their common cause.

Once that great goal is achieved, they well understand that it is not they who will benefit: it will be the young people of Scotland. It will be for the young people of Scotland to make a free Scotland a long-term working reality. It will be for the young people of Scotland to mould a bright and better future for their own children and grandchildren, and all the generations to come. But first we need to achieve independence.

The case for independence is what this book is all about. It is imbued with urgency and enthusiasm. But it is most definitely NOT about what precisely would happen in an independent Scotland, because nobody knows. That is the whole point. The people of Scotland would at long last be empowered to decide what their country was to be like and the direction it was to take. At the beginning, there would be an open book. So it is not the purpose of this book to discuss exactly what an independent Scotland would and would not do.

Those who are now youngsters in today's Scotland will be resolving such matters and questions in the years to come. The authors of this book are fully aware that the blossoming of an independent Scotland will be a long process. They will not live to see the all the fruits of the confidence, the empowering, the freedom. But that does not stop their fervent wish to achieve for Scots in the centuries to come this grandest and most exciting of opportunities. For what can be more exciting than a nation starting afresh, and getting the chance to fulfil its aspirations, dreams and visions?

It is however more than an opportunity, however grand. It is also a responsibility. Moulding the future is work that is challenging and responsible as well as heady and invigorating.

History will be made, not just in the achievement of independence, but in all the months and years ahead as the new state rolls out its policies and its programmes.

There is no naïve suggestion in this book that an independent Scotland would be operating in some benign vacuum. No modern nation state can be truly, purely independent in a world that is predicated on interdependency as never before. Transnational institutions have enormous importance. It is folly to claim that any nation-state can operate in glorious isolation.

But then that is not the sort of claim our five authors make. They are rather writing about something that is honourable and just; the need for a nation, a proud and historic nation, to fulfil its potential as a state as well. It is wrong that a nation like Scotland, known the world over, should have been subsumed for so long into a much larger state. Scotland, at present, finds itself in the sad limbo of stateless nationhood.

The other crucial point for readers to note is that this book is in no way infused with anti-English sentiment. Far from it. Each of the authors, in their various distinctive ways, believes that an independent Scotland would actually be good for England. Each of them sincerely wishes England well.

Meanwhile the first the great step, at once simple, historic and momentous, has to be taken, and that is to achieve independence. This book is about that inescapable imperative.

CHAPTER 1

Make a Noble Dream Come True

HARRY REID

A Romp Through 301 Years

THE CASE FOR SCOTTISH independence is a most positive one. The latter (and shorter) part of this essay will therefore be very positive. But there is also a strong argument for Scottish independence that is essentially negative, and I wish to deal with this first.

This negative case is predicated on the fact that the Union between England and Scotland in 1707 created the British state, and the British state is clearly in terminal decay. It is not working; it is not serving its people adequately. Many of its citizens are unaware of any meaningful concept of British nationhood. Far less do they believe in any such concept. Meanwhile the leaders of the UK are essentially engaged in the management of decline and they are not even very good at that. The break-up of the British state would give Scotland a splendid chance to regroup, to renew, to build and to roll out an improving and forward-looking society. And that applies to England, too.

Yet many people wish to cling onto the British state. This suggests a failure of vision, certainly a failure of imagination. It also speaks of a mixture of complacency, conservatism, fear of change and timidity, which in turn perhaps reflects the rather cowed condition of a state mired in incompetence and full of doubt and even shame.

In its early days, in the 18th century, the British state was characterised by venality, duplicity and incompetence on a spectacular scale. The terms of the Union itself were broken early on: for example, Scottish landowners were given the right to appoint parish ministers, a breach of the Union settlement which to many Scots was contentious, offensive and provocative. How could this happen in direct contravention of the Union agreement? The answer is that the English had in effect taken over Scotland.

The man who to all intents dominated the British state in its early years was the first British prime minister. An Englishman called Sir Robert Walpole, he was an egregious rogue, one of the most corrupt political leaders in European history. Most of his successors were, if not as corrupt, weak and incompetent.

Among the 'achievements' of the British state in its first century was the repression of the Scottish Highlands after the failed Jacobite rebellion of 1745–6. The majority of Scots did not support the Jacobites, but the post-Culloden breaking up of Scottish Highland society was unnecessarily vicious and vindictive. Another 'achievement' was the loss of the American colonies. The British state wanted to retain these colonies and their loss was a debacle characterised by serial political bungling and compounded by crass military incompetence.

In the latter part of the century the early stirrings of industrialisation anticipated the huge social and economic revolution which made Britain the manufacturing centre of the entire world. This was partly the consequence of superb natural resources in Scotland and England, especially the rich coalfields, and the emergence of a breed of brilliant engineers, inventors and entrepreneurs, some of them men of little education who excelled at improvisation. One such was the canal builder of genius James Brindley who revolutionised the internal transport system through much of England. Many of these remarkable figures were Scots.

The Union had undoubtedly provided a significant tariff-free internal market, while the nascent Empire was to provide further economic opportunity abroad. But at the same time the social consequences of all this, not least mass migration to ill planned new cities, were often catastrophic. The industrial revolution, as it came to be called, was blemished by the systematic exploitation of very cheap labour. The British state was for at least three generations utterly unable to deal with the social effects of the creation of the first large-scale modern proletariat.

As well as inventors, industrialists and engineers of genius, Britain was producing outstanding thinkers, writers and reformers. Scotland provided more than her fair share of this special breed. A topical exemplar was Adam Smith, the Scottish philosopher and economist who was perhaps the supreme theorist of markets and capitalism.

Also in the ranks of these thinkers and writers were many radical and far-sighted subversives. Too often, if understandably, the British state regarded them as enemies. An example was Tom Paine, who played a significant role in both the American and French revolutions and to this day remains a hero in the US and France. (In Britain he is virtually forgotten – the British have to a large extent lost their sense of history).

Paine was tried in Britain, though he was exiled, for sedition. The British state was determined to crush him. The chief prosecutor, a future British prime minister, described Paine as wicked and malicious. The jury, picked by the Government, did not even bother to hear the judge's summing up, they were so eager to pronounce Paine guilty. He was sentenced to death. Such bitterly inglorious episodes were all too common.

Eventually, in the Victorian era, there was at last a realistic state response to the colossal social evils created by massive and rapid industrialisation. It was a miracle that there had not been a full scale revolution.

Meanwhile the British Empire was stretching across the globe. I do not want to get into the debate about whether the British were good or bad imperialists. The audit on the imperial legacy must be mixed. But two points are crucial. It was not an unmitigated success, and the legacy is often depressing.

For example if we look at two rogue states which are causing much anguish in the world today because of their reckless disregard for civilised behaviour to their own citizens – Zimbabwe and Burma – we can see the grievous long-term consequences of failed British imperialism. Secondly, the spectacular speed at which the Empire was lost in the second part of the 20th century was a major contributor to a loss of self-confidence in Britishness, though this was perhaps less of a factor in Scotland.

The early years of the 20th century were marked by the eminently avoidable disaster of the First World War, which was a catastrophe for Britain. Many of its best young men did not return from four years of pointless carnage. Those who did return from the 'war to end all wars' did not come back to a land fit for heroes. They returned to a state which was torn apart by industrial strife, including the first general strike, ever rising unemployment and increasing social faction and division.

Indeed I would argue that the British state only really came good in the middle of the 20th century, when there were two significant, and in different ways glorious, developments. Galvanised by a one-off war leader of unsurpassed genius, Winston Churchill, the British people defied the unique and heinous menace of Nazism, and for a time stood alone against that evil. When the Nazi war machine had at last been defeated (not least by the Americans and the Russians), the British state was exhausted.

Then came the second development, in its different way almost as remarkable. Despite its impoverished post-war condition, the British people found the courage to embark on a huge social experiment, the creation of a colossal 'welfare state'. The guiding genius was the Liberal politician William Beveridge, who wanted to eliminate the giant evils he identified in British society: Want, Disease, Ignorance, Squalor and Idleness. It was a vastly expensive and nobly motivated experiment, all the more impressive for being launched by a state that was virtually bankrupt after a heroic war effort.

The experiment has been at best a mixed success. On many tests, not least the elimination of Beveridge's five evils, it has been a failure. Nonetheless when it was launched by the socialist government of Clem Attlee, it was a brave and progressive experiment. Professor Tom Devine has argued that in

Scotland the introduction of interventionist social policies guaranteeing decent standards of living helped to mitigate the effects of loss of Empire. The welfare state became the defining essence of the British state.

Thus the 1940s were a remarkable decade, and for me these years marked the last high point of Britishness. The magnificent generation who were in their prime then have been sadly passing away. This is of great significance when we observe the contemporary crisis of the British state. The fact that many of the generation who fought the war and created our welfare state are now dead while those of them who are still alive are seniors and will not be with us for much longer has profound significance.

These are the people for whom the Union had a particular resonance; the 'think of what we've all been through together' generation. For many of them, the British state is understandably something to be proud of. And again for them, two components of the British state, the monarchy and the armed forces, have especial emotional resonance.

But in the 1950s a rapid decline set in. Britain became much less important in the world, even in Europe. The British state was not just losing its Empire; its great wartime ally, the US, was increasingly indifferent; and the rising states of the new Europe were aloof and disdainful.

The British state did maintain its supposedly independent nuclear deterrent which guaranteed it a place at the world's top table, via permanent membership of the UN Security Council, but that merely masked (very expensively) the reality of pervasive decline. Further, the main base for the 'deterrent' was in Scotland, which made Scotland a prime target during the Cold War.

There was in the 1950s and even more obviously in the 1960s, a failure of national confidence. British nationhood became something to be scorned and mocked rather than admired. The slick Tory showman Harold Macmillan preached a cynical consumerist paean to brittle short term affluence ('You've never had it so good' was his most famous, or rather infamous, slogan) in order to disguise the loss of power, esteem and national confidence. Socially the British became less cohesive; satire and permissiveness undermined what older citizens regarded, vaguely, as core British values.

The first great shock to British self-esteem had come with the Suez debacle of 1956; many more were to follow. Six of the leading countries on the continent formed the European Common Market; Britain first stayed aloof, and then desperately tried to join, only to be snubbed by the French. This was a terrible blow to British *amour propre*, if that is the appropriate phrase.

In the 1970s several eminent and distinguished observers thought Britain was becoming ungovernable. In 1976 the Labour government so mismanaged the British state's finances that it had to borrow, in humiliating desperation, huge amounts of money from the International Monetary Fund and from West Germany. This was at the very time when North Sea oil revenues were beginning to cascade into the British state's coffers. The paradox was not lost on many perceptive Scots. The slogan 'It's Scotland's oil' had a potent and legitimate resonance.

At this time a group of Scottish Nationalist MPs had been elected to the Westminster. Parliament. One of them, the redoubtable Winnie Ewing, later described most of the Unionist MPs who were representing Scottish seats as boorish mediocrities. She was especially contemptuous of the Labour MPs. 'I'd look at the ranks of these people in the debating chamber. I thought: My God, these people are representing my country, they are representing Scotland. In these days many Labour activists in Scotland, and even more Labour voters, were decent hardworking people. Yet the people they elected were often third-raters'.

I think her strictures are justified, though I'm sure that at least some of the Scottish Labour MPs were decent, industrious politicians. One such was Frank McElhone, who represented the Gorbals area in Glasgow. I got to know him well when I was working as an education journalist; Frank was for a time Scottish education minister in the Callaghan government.

Publicly, Frank always averred that Labour would deliver for the people of Scotland; privately he was less certain.

He told me more than once that he feared for the future of the city he loved, Glasgow. He believed that there was what he called a diaspora of the 'virile working class' (Frank was never politically correct) to the various Scottish new towns. He feared that many of the families left in Glasgow would break up, and many of its citizens – hundreds of thousands of them – would become wholly dependent on the state.

Yet he conceded that the state could never sustain all these people's needs. He set up a kind of one-off, supercharged citizens' support bureau, known as Frank's Bank, in the Gorbals, partly to cut through state bureaucracy. He believed passionately in the welfare state; at the same time he admitted that for many of his constituents, it wasn't delivering.

Meanwhile in London one of the most able of the Nationalist MPs, the late Douglas Henderson, was asked to characterise how the two great Unionist parties, the Tories and Labour, reacted to a well organised group of Nats at Westminster. He replied in one word: 'Horror'.

The Labour Government of the late 1970s not only grievously mishandled Britain's finances; it also presided over a calamitous collapse in industrial relations. Public strife escalated, culminating in the 'winter of discontent' when, at one point, the dead were not buried.

This spiral of political and economic decline was partly reversed by the belated arrival of a strong leader, Margaret Thatcher; the most significant figure by far in the recent history of the British state. She had many impressive qualities, not least courage and conviction, compared to her predecessors Callaghan, Wilson, Heath, Douglas Home, Macmillan and Eden, who were all essentially third or fourth-rate leaders, but she was also a disastrously divisive force within the British state.

In Scotland she was detested. She was perceived as anti-Scottish, a view that was compounded when Scotland was selected as a kind of testing ground for her hated 'poll tax'. Whether she meant to or not, she did enormous damage to the already fragile cohesion of the British state. In Scotland, respect for and belief in the Union was now more strained than ever.

It was in 1979 that Margaret Thatcher became leader of a state that appeared near to breakdown. She applied much tough medicine to the confused and stricken patient but she was in no way a gentle or caring physician.

All this meant that the concept of 'Britishness' was becoming almost impossible to nurture. As noted above, one or two British institutions – notably the monarchy and our armed forces – still held an emotional resonance for many older British citizens in a way that seemed to endorse British values as being decent, strong and worthy of patriotic pride.

But other British institutions, including the Westminster Parliament itself, were regarded with growing contempt. When the precocious Scottish Labour politician Gordon Brown, who was later to become a beleaguered and inept leader of the British state, was desperately looking for something to serve as a benign and positive focus for Britishness, he seized on the National Health Service, the key component in the welfare state that had been created in the 1940s. It was significant that he did not refer to the British Parliament which had been created so many years earlier.

That most perceptive of contemporary journalists, Neal Ascherson, has closely observed these eddies and tides in the affairs of the British state. In his 2006 Orwell Lecture Ascherson reflected on how Gordon Brown, as we have just seen, seized on the National Health Service as 'a common achievement, a great moral reform' as he searched for a fitting object of British patriotism. Ascherson claimed that this was actually the most impressive thought Brown had ever put forward. But he went on to note that in a later interview with the right-wing *Daily Telegraph*, Brown praised the British patriotism of Churchill and Thatcher – but nobody in his own party.

He celebrated 'British virtue' as 'liberty married to social responsibility and a belief in what Churchill called fair play'. Ascherson, then wryly noted that this was 'attractive, but not solid enough to form the pedestal for a new patriotism'.

I personally believe that any meaningful notion of British patriotism is now virtually defunct. Yet the idea of Scottish patriotism, and indeed the idea of English patriotism, are both alive and well. They could and should be harnessed by benign and progressive politicians.

This romp through the 301 years of 'British' history is a story of both significant achievement and appalling defeat. It is a narrative marked by interludes of glory, but marred by persistent failure and growing decline. I have tried to be careful to give the English their due; they are in so many ways a magnificent people. They have produced more than their fair share of geniuses and authentic world figures. Shakespeare and Newton must surely be among the handful of utterly momentous world-changing, world-enhancing human beings.

Further, the authors of the many problems of the British state have been Scottish as well as English. Many Scottish politicians in both the Labour and Tory parties have over the years been culpable, in that they have directly contributed to the decline of the British state, whose main hallmark is now a corrosive and constant incompetence.

I have above cited as examples of British individual greatness the engineer Brindley, the writer and thinker Paine, the war leader Churchill; this is not to defer to the English, but rather to indicate that they have consistently produced men and women of genius who have contributed enormously to the British state, and beyond. Whatever this essay is about, it is not about any glib anti-Englishness, any disdain for English achievement.

But since the 1950s Britain has produced far fewer outstanding individuals and, as I have tried to indicate, the British state has become mired in decline. The decay noticeably set in at the time of the Suez fiasco and has been accelerating ever since. My contention is simple: the British state is spent.

On the other hand I do not wish to exaggerate; British citizens still live in a free and relatively stable society. But they are not as confident, happy, prosperous and ambitious as they should and could be. They are less well educated than they might be; their behaviour is increasingly self indulgent, anarchic and turbulent; and their future looks problematic. Too many of them are almost encouraged by the state to leech off that very state; Britain has a huge number of young people who are not in education, employment or training. Others, often those at the bottom of the heap, are given scant support or assistance by the state in their daily struggle.

Obviously constitutional change cannot of itself solve these issues, but it can act as an enabler. It can provide the platform for significant revival.

Before I move on to the more positive part of this essay I wish to return briefly to our British armed forces. As I have suggested, they are one of the few remaining authentic causes for real pride in Britishness. We have a world class military, but more and more they are being betrayed by their political masters. How has the British state treated them, the people who ultimately are trained to kill and to lay down their lives to defend us?

In one word, despicably.

In the past 10 years alone the British state has made enormous demands on its military, particularly in Kosovo, Sierra Leone, Afghanistan and Iraq. Despite this commitment, and the consequent acute overstretch, that state has spent less and less on the military as a percentage of the British national income. (Quite the opposite is true in areas like health and education, with distinctly mixed results).

Our troops have been sent into action with inadequate back up. Already in dangerous theatres, they have been placed in even more peril because of faulty equipment. There have been casualties that have been eminently avoidable. Further the support for the troops' families in crucial areas such as housing has been dire.

To make this even worse, at least one of the wars, the invasion of Iraq and the consequent fighting there, was both illegal and mounted on an utterly bogus pretext. This points to moral bankruptcy at the very heart of the British state.

Further, I simply cannot believe that an independent Scottish state would ever send its troops to invade a far-off land in an illegal military adventure spuriously based on 'sexed-up' intelligence. I may be ingenuous in writing that. But I prefer to think that I am simply being realistic.

To make all this even worse still, the British state has shown contempt for the proud military traditions of Scotland by its irresponsible treatment of illustrious Scottish regiments.

In other words, the British state can no longer be trusted to take our defence or our history seriously. Instead it has engaged in dubious foreign adventures, and at the same time it has systematically abused its duty of care and succour to the military.

In the light of all the above, I think the case for the Union is sketchy, to put it mildly. Indeed because it is failing its citizens, I believe that we have a moral as well as a political duty to break it up.

I accept that the Scottish and English people have been part of it for more than 300 years, and over this long period a certain attachment has inevitably developed. There is always the 'aye been' tendency. Many people are conservative, and are often scared of change. They are used to the Union, and they may to some extent have been persuaded that those who wish to break up the Union are a dangerous collection of zealots, unworldly intellectuals and sentimentalists. But such frivolous fears and diversions are essentially deceitful. And there is another side to the debate: the authentic, positive vision for Scottish independence, to which I now turn.

The Vision – Looking ahead to an independent, international Scotland

In political terms, Independence means two very different things. First, it means the right of a nation state to govern itself in its own land and sea; its legal right to do so would be endorsed by international law. This means that no other state

– even a relatively benign neighbour – has any right to interfere in the internal affairs of that the independent country. This is the independence that I want, fervently, Scotland to achieve, the sooner the better.

There is a second, more problematic version of independence. This implies freedom from dependence on any other power, organisation or state. In this sense, no state, not even the most overweening and seemingly powerful, ever achieves perfect independence. To compound this reality, we now live in a complex world of instant global communication and ever-growing interdependability. It is also a world of many supranational organisations, such as the European Union.

To be fair to the Scottish National Party, it has generally been sensible in its understanding of this second type of independence. The party has usually and honourably conceded that in this world of global connections, perfect independence is just a chimera.

Mention of the Scottish National Party, incidentally, points to a tactical difficulty. It has undoubtedly been the main means of articulating the case for Scottish independence, and it has done so doggedly and decently, sometimes in the face of disgraceful attacks from Unionist parties. (Of course some Unionist politicians, Labour and Tory, detest the idea of independence because it could ruin their political careers, rendering them redundant.)

At the same time it has to be admitted that the SNP's growing and impressive electoral (and now administrative) success is not necessarily predicated on the imperative of independence. The party has undoubtedly been used by many Scottish voters to make a short term point; for example by those who have wished to hurt Labour without voting Conservative. But because it has been used by tactical voters does not in any way vitiate its essential integrity. For a nationalist party, it has been a model of responsibility, probity and restraint.

This takes us directly on to nationalism, for as well as the idea of independence, there is, obviously enough, the concomitant notion of nationalism. This is more sensitive, for nationalism can obviously be abused. (As I say, it has NOT been abused by Scotland's own nationalist party). At its narrowest, nationalism can take the form of diseased ethnocentricity – us against the world – or a kind of racist exclusion of those who do not belong to the pure nation. These perversions of nationalism are abhorrent. But at its best nationalism celebrates the linking of state to nation, and vice versa. This means that Scotland's current plight is most unfortunate. It is a proud, historic nation that is subsumed into a bigger, and failing, state.

A confident nation can and should nurture a confident patriotism. This is nothing to do with any puffed up notions of superiority, which admittedly the Scots occasionally indulge in ('Wha's like us?') but rather a respect for and pride in a rich history, culture and physicality (and Scotland's landscape is especially varied and beautiful). It should involve a judicious but strong appreciation of past and present achievements. In Scottish history, there are so many achievements that one book could not begin to deal with them all. There are also many failures and things to be ashamed of; that should not be forgotten. But looking ahead, there should also be an aspirational component in patriotism that takes it far beyond mere nostalgia or sentiment. True patriots should revere much of the past; but they are always looking forward. And at this particular time, Scots have unusually good reasons to be looking ahead. We have the opportunity, quite simply, to recreate our country; to be born again.

This accords with the aspirational aspect of patriotism. To love your country is nothing to be ashamed of; indeed it is a noble thing. It need not and should not imply aggressiveness or belligerence to outsiders. Chauvinism is bad; patriotism is good. And what better way to express patriotism than to set free a nation that for too long has been annexed by another, larger state? Set it free, and rebuild it. That is the task before us.

Meanwhile the Scottish nation has survived in many respects so that its recovery of independence need not be at all difficult or complex. Scotland may within living memory have enjoyed less autonomy over its own affairs than some English local authorities, but it has been lucky in that it was able to maintain many distinctive institutions such as its own legal system, its own education system and its own national church, the Church of Scotland.

Indeed the latter, in its annual general assembly, an enormously impressive week-long event held in Edinburgh each year and attended by around 1,000 'commissioners' from presbyteries and parishes the length and breadth of Scotland, was perhaps the nearest the Scottish nation had to its own parliament in the years between 1707 and 1999, when the devolved Parliament at Holyrood at last came into being.

So if Scotland's parliament disappeared into the mists of the Union in 1707, other institutions were able to maintain a rigorous and codified Scottishness. Further, the Scottish system of local government was very different from the English one. But it was in Scots law, a genuinely national system of both criminal and civil law with its own courts and judges, and many exceptionally distinguished jurists, that Scotland most effectively maintained a distinctive and separate entity that could one day be one of the building blocks of an independent Scotland. And of course there are many other separate Scottish institutions, not least the Scottish media and Scottish sporting bodies, though sadly some of these have gone into a decline (which could well, though not inevitably, be revived by independence).

It is then happy and fortunate that a framework for the new Scottish state is to some extent already in existence. But that is hardly the essence of the vision for independence, to which I at last turn.

Of Course We Can

Elsewhere in this book there is a great deal of hard detail about the feasibility of independence. Here I'd prefer to prosecute a more idealistic, even visionary, case.

When I was a young journalist I had the privilege of getting to know the great radical educationist R. F. Mackenzie. The son of a stationmaster in the heart of Aberdeenshire, Mackenzie was a man of many parts. In the 1930s, when he was in his 20s, he travelled all over Europe by bicycle, and taught in both Germany and Switzerland. In the war he served as navigator with Bomber Command. Then he resumed his teaching career, and eventually he was appointed headmaster of a comprehensive school on a big housing estate on the western outskirts of Aberdeen.

There he pursued his child-centred vision of a more enlightened approach to state education. But his ideas were far too wild for the councillors of Aberdeen, his employers, though they had appointed him in the full knowledge that he was unlikely to be an orthodox or a conservative head. He was suspended – in effect fired – in April 1974, when he was 63. The debate that took place before Aberdeen Education Committee took their fateful decision was long, bitter and contentious. When Mackenzie himself addressed his employers, the tone suddenly became elevated. His speech was the most eloquent and moving I have ever heard. But his words were to no avail.

The next day Scotland's leading tabloid newspaper, the *Daily Record*, accused those who had suspended him of treachery. Mackenzie, a brilliant man who had an immense amount to offer Scotland was left sidelined and disgruntled. Is it fanciful to suggest that this debacle would not have occurred in an independent Scotland? Well, I'm certain that a free Scotland would have found a positive way of harnessing this exceptional man's idealism and aspiration.

A few hours after the meeting when Mackenzie was suspended and in effect discarded by his country, I spent several hours talking with him in his farmhouse by the River Dee. I had several more long chats with him, but it was that first conversation, which lasted into the small hours, that I remember best. He was a man of the far left and I would place myself on the near right, but increasingly I became convinced by his vision and his dream, always articulated fluently and without the slightest pomposity. He had a lovely gentle way of talking in his soft Aberdeenshire accent, mixing English and Scots words constantly.

I was delighted when he asked me to write the introduction to his book *The Unbowed Head*. Looking back, I think there were two key points in his idea of a better Scotland.

The first was his insistence that Scotland's most important resource was not its oil but its young people. He expressed this view forcefully at the very time when North Sea oil was becoming a hot political issue, and Aberdeen itself was booming as never before. He believed passionately that far too many young Scots were not being properly brought up, and were most certainly not being properly educated.

He had long, bruising experience of edgy, suspicious, difficult Scottish children, lacking in confidence and unaware of their own potential, far more sure about what they did not want to do than what they could do. If it was bad then, over 30 years ago, it is far worse now. Mackenzie fervently wished to create a society that would unleash these young people's goodness, their capacity to better themselves and others.

His second key point was that the political process all over the world, in democracies and totalitarian states alike, had been abrogated by elite, arrogant, self-serving minorities. In the British context he was particularly angry with the Labour Party, which he thought was betraying the ideals of its founders.

I cannot remember his exact words to me, but they were along these lines: If every Scottish individual can achieve genuine independence, our country will be truly independent.

He believed with extraordinary passion in the ability of Scots to run their own affairs; at the same time he was deeply suspicious of many of the leaders of his own profession, teaching. He was even more disillusioned with power brokers like trade union leaders and civil servants and businessmen and lawyers and, yes, politicians. Mackenzie saw the role of politicians as being enablers, not rulers.

The man confused me. At times he seemed impossibly unworldly, yet his analysis accorded in many ways with my own, more tentative, efforts to understand my country. I had always felt that Scotland was good at producing individuals who excelled, but less good at producing the back-up and succour for those who were not obviously able and industrious. Those who displayed enterprise, and there were plenty of them, were often less good at fostering it in others. As a nation we had never seemed particularly proficient at working together, or even tolerating each other.

Of course Mackenzie was derided for being impossibly ingenuous, an innocent at large in a complex world dominated by transnational forces of mega-power and big business. His detractors would sometimes sneer that he had big ideas aplenty, but he had no notion of politics, not even educational politics. Others would point out that he had not even been able to run his own school properly. To some extent this was true; he claimed he had been given a divided staff, but it is undeniable that he could not carry all his staff with him.

But I think the huge importance of Mackenzie was that he articulated an unusually noble dream of a better Scotland. It would be based, above all else, on belief in and support for the country's young. Too many of them, he claimed, had wounds in their souls. It would be difficult for them to be good people. good parents, good citizens.

As I listened to Mackenzie, I often thought: Here is a prophet; here is a man who has so much to offer his country. But his country in effect spat him out. Of course someone like Mackenzie would always be difficult to work with and would need a sympathetic and understanding context in which to operate. It is my belief that Scotland teems with such people; they are not always easy people, but a progressive, free country would allow them scope. It would never hold them back.

Mackenzie's own father was apparently a difficult man. As a youngster he was embarrassed when he heard his dad arguing vehemently with courteous and kind neighbours. The young R. F. Mackenzie sought friendship and reassurance and he did not always receive those from his father. At the same time he could respect his father's integrity and his will.

What we need in Scotland is the ability to give people the

opportunities and the support systems and the frameworks they need, so that grim integrity and generous friendship do not collide, as the boy Mackenzie witnessed them colliding. Equally we must allow those with vision to pursue their dreams; we must succour and sustain them, not mock or discard them.

Many – possibly most – of us Scots nurture our own dream of a better Scotland. The point about independence is not that we would immediately be able to see our own personal dreams come to fruition; of course not. But independence would be the great enabler, the springboard to allow us at least to try.

I do not see an independent Scotland as some kind of social laboratory, but I do see it as an open-minded and ameliorative state that would harness our country's terrific tradition of democratic idealism and long, noble belief in education – both of these go back for at least four centuries – and self-improvement. At the same time we could nurture our considerable awkward squad, all our iconoclasts and visionaries and free thinkers. We would never be beholden to self-serving careerists, or the tired satraps of the declining British state.

We may have lost our way somewhat – R.F. Mackenzie suggested to me that we are totally lost – but the right way can be found easily enough, and we are on the brink of finding it. All we need is the freedom to do it our way. That is what this is all about. The idea is simple yet challenging: it is about finding the right route twice, finding the correct way forward, but in our own way.

When Scotland is independent, we shall owe much to the politicians who have taken us to that happy state. But from then on it will up to all of us to create the new, better Scotland. We will not be able to blame others, we will no longer be held back by the decay of the British state. More importantly, we could all work together. Can we? To paraphrase Senator Obama, of course we can,

All we need is the opportunity. At long last, that huge, glorious opportunity is within sight, within our very grasp. If we have the courage.

CHAPTER 2

Independence is the Answer

PAUL HENDERSON SCOTT

IN HIS CELEBRATED BOOK, *Small is Beautiful,* E. F. Schumacher challenged the theory in which he had been brought up. That was the belief that 'in order to be prosperous a country had to be big – the bigger the better'. On the contrary he found that 'if we make a list of all the most prosperous countries in the world, we find that most of them are very small; whereas a list of the biggest countries in the world shows most of them to be very poor indeed... In the actual world there is a tremendous longing and striving to profit, if at all possible, from the convenience, humanity and manageability of smallness'[1].

Schumacher's point is confirmed by the latest available statistics for the countries of the European Union. They show that the six most prosperous are small:-

	GDP per head. (in purchasing power standard)	Population (in millions)
Luxembourg	58,900	0.5
Ireland	32,600	4.2
Netherlands	29,500	16.3
Austria	28,900	8.3
Denmark	28,600	5.4
Belgium	27,700	10.5

They are followed by the UK with a GDP per head of 27,700 and a population of 60.4 million; but Luxembourg the smallest is also by far the most prosperous[2].

Long before Schumacher, others had reached the same conclusion, including two of the key figures of the Scottish Enlightenment. David Hume in his essay, *Idea of a Perfect*

Commonwealth said: 'A small commonwealth is the happiest government in the world, within itself, because everything lies under the eye of the rulers'[3]. Adam Ferguson in *An Essay on the History of Civil Society* of 1767, wrote of the advantages of living in society and added:

> We need not enlarge our communities in order to enjoy these advantages. We frequently obtain them the most remarkable degree, where nations remain independent, and are of small extent[4].

Both Hume and Ferguson were, of course, writing only a few decades after Scotland had lost her independence in the Union of 1707.

In recent years, particularly since the end of the Second World War, there has been a rapid increase in the number of small states. The present is the Age of Liberation (the title of my recent book) in which nearly all of the multi-national states and the empires have dissolved into their component parts. When Schumacher published *Small is Beautiful* in 1947 he said 'The United Nations Organisation started some 25 years ago with some 60 members; now there are more than twice as many, and the number is still growing'[5]. With the recent addition of Montenegro, a few weeks after a successful referendum on independence, there are now 192.

As it happens, I have been able to witness the progress which has been achieved by two of these new states since they became independent. I have been lecturing on cruises to the Baltic and have visited Estonia several times. Slovenian PEN holds an annual conference of writers which is so interesting, welcoming and friendly that participation each year has become an addiction. The change in both of these countries since they became independent has been dramatic. Not only have they become rapidly much more prosperous, but also unmistakably more self-confident, optimistic and quite simply happier.

The Scottish Enlightenment invented the idea, which was later adopted in the American Declaration of Independence, that the object of government is the pursuit of happiness. Estonia and Slovenia have demonstrated it in practice. In my years as a diplomat I visited many countries and I have always had the impression that small countries were happier than the large. It is probably because the smaller are more homogeneous and their governments are closer to the people and have an easier task in meeting their wishes and needs. Norway is a small country which became independent from Sweden just over a century ago and is now one of the most prosperous and contented in the world. A Norwegian professor at the University of Oslo, Johan P. Olsen, has said the following of the advantages of the small states:

> Many smaller European states have a good historical record when it comes to democratic development, peaceful co-existence, prosperity, welfare, equality between social classes, districts and gender, life expectancy, cultural development and ecological consciousness. A democratic argument has been that the political community has to be small in order for citizens to have insight, participation, influence and a feeling of belonging and trust.

He adds that in this globalised world small states have more experience than the larger of coping with events over which they have no control and are therefore better in responding to them[6].

In his contribution to this book Tom Nairn also discusses the advantages which small nations have in responding to the challenges of a globalised world. They also benefit from the increased role of international organisations such as the United Nations and the European Union. Their effect is to curb the power of the large countries and increase the influence of the small. Several heads of government of the smaller members of the European Union have made this point. For instance Poul Schluter, when he was Prime Minister of Denmark, said:

> I feel a lot more powerful than a Danish Prime Minister would have felt years ago. Why? Because under all circumstances this is a rather small neighbouring country

> to Germany and the strong economy. In the old days, we just had to accept any steps taken in the German economy, and its consequences on us. Nowadays, my ministers and I take part in the Council of Ministers meetings in Europe. We have influence, and a lot more influence than is fair,considering that we are such a small nation[7].

Garret Fitzgerald, a former Prime Minister of Ireland, in a speech in 1989:

> Over a period of many years, I have come to the paradoxical conclusion that it is in the process of merging its sovereignty with other Member States in the Community that Ireland has found the clearest 'ex post facto' justification for its long struggle to achieve independence from the United Kingdom[8].

Mary Robinson, when she was President of Ireland, said in a speech when she was on a visit to Scotland in June 1992:

> There has been a great sense of liberation. We have become more sure of our own Irish identity in the context of being equal partners in Europe. It meant that we no longer simply define ourselves in terms of our relationship with Britain.
>
> We are Irish but we are also European... Ireland and Scotland have much in common yet there are very few institutional links that recognise this. We must build them up[9].

The Disadvantages of the Union

The historian, Hume Brown said of the Union of the Crowns of 1603, when James VI of Scotland became also James I of England:

> The Union of the crowns brought many disadvantages to Scotland, but the result of it that most vitally affected

> her was her severance from the nations at a period when new principles and new ideas were guiding their policy.
>
> Throughout the entire century Scotland was a severed and withered branch, and her people knew it[10].

This was a time when the existence of a nation and the conduct of its foreign policy were closely identified with the monarch. The countries of Europe, which were accustomed to dealing with an independent Scotland, now had the impression that it had been absorbed by England. This view was confirmed by the parliamentary union of 1707. The English Parliament was to continue as before, except only for the addition of very few Scottish members. In the Commons of 558 members Scotland was to have 45, only one more than the county of Cornwall. In the Lords there would be only 16 Scottish peers, although the Church of England alone had 26 bishops. It is not surprising that the rest of Europe refused to be deceived by the adoption of the new term, Britain. Even our oldest ally, France, stuck like the others to their word for England. That was a recognition of the reality.

A small country in a union with a larger one, such as Scotland with England, is always at a disadvantage. Inevitably the larger country is likely to put its own interests first, and react to the ideas and attitudes of their own people, in preference to those of the smaller. In fact, it could be said that this is democratically proper because the views of the majority should prevail. Scotland is a country which evolved over centuries of independent history. For much of this time Scotland was in much closer contact, politically, culturally and intellectually, with other countries in Europe than with England. Even after the Union the church, the law, education, literature and music remained distinct from those of England. It is therefore not surprising that Scottish ideas and aspirations, politically and culturally are often very different from those of England.

An important example of this is in attitudes to international affairs. The majority view in England evidently is that the country should still aspire to the role of a great power. It is presumably for this reason that the UK Government clings to nuclear weapons and regards itself as the major ally of the United States. In fact, that makes it more of a puppet than a partner. This has led to British involvement in the illegal and disastrous Iraq war and the encouragement of terrorism. The majority of Scots are opposed to nuclear weapons and would prefer to see Scotland playing a co-operative, rational and peaceful role in the world.

Some opponents of Scottish independence are given to asking in an incredulous tone, as if it was self-evidently absurd, 'a Scottish diplomatic service, army, navy and airforce?' Of course, many countries in Europe which are smaller than Scotland, maintain all of these things of a scale and nature which are perfectly adequate for their needs. An independent Scotland could easily do the same. They would cost less than the contribution which Scotland makes through UK taxation to inflated ideas of Britain's role in the world. These forces would be appropriate to our needs and, like our own diplomatic service, would not be distracted by other objectives.

Many Scots are astonished and exasperated by the way some people in England cling to this absurd notion of the country as still a great and imperial power free from the restraints of international organisations. The novelist, Iain Banks, expressed this in an interview with the *Edinburgh Evening News:*

> I'm at the stage of thinking we have to leave England to its fate. If it wants to leave the EU, then let it stew in its own past imperial dreamland. Scotland can be a great small country in Europe. We can make a success of it and be a more humane society than this privatised and selfishness oriented country[11].

Nuclear Submarines

The British Government has not only insisted on retaining and renewing nuclear-armed submarines, but on stationing them on the Clyde, close to our largest centre of population. This is a violation of obligations under the treaty against the proliferation of nuclear weapons and tends to encourage other countries to follow this bad example. They present a permanent risk of a catastrophic accident or terrorist attack. They are not, as they are described, an 'independent deterrent' because they are dependent on American co-operation. Also they serve no real purpose. At the time of the Cold War, the submarines cruised with their nuclear weapons targeted at sites in the Soviet Union. Where are they targeted now? The official estimate of the cost of renewing these submarines is £15 to 20 billion. Other estimates are even higher. As long as the Union continues, about a 10th of this would fall on the Scottish taxpayer. If we deny the use of the Clyde base, either through ending the Union or in some other interim way, it would be difficult to find an English constituency that would be prepared to tolerate the submarines on their doorstep. If that were to lead to the abandonment of the whole project that would be of benefit to us all.

Scottish Oil

Another very obvious disadvantage of the Union is the assumption, or seizure, by the British Government of the revenue from the oil in Scottish waters.

When the oil was discovered in the 1970s a senior Treasury official said in a memorandum to ministers:

> It is conceivable that income per head in Scotland could be 25 per cent or 30 per cent higher than that prevailing in England during the 1980s, given independence[12].

Since this was obviously a strong argument for Scottish independence ministers of both Conservative and Labour Governments did their best to confuse the issue by concealing the great potential value of the oil reserves. In fact their value in the last six years alone has been £38 billion and the official estimate is that it will be about £55 billion over the next five or six years. With such wealth under the control of an independent Scotland, we could, like Norway, build up a reserve fund to guarantee our prosperity for the indefinite future. And, of course, this is an asset which has grown enormously in value with the steady increase in the price of oil.

The Need for Scottish Membership of the European Union

Another major disadvantage of the Union is that it denies Scotland our own membership of the international organisations, especially the European Union. British representatives to it generally ignore Scottish interests or views when they differ from those of England. The senior Scottish official in our European office, Michael Avon, made this very clear in a letter to the then Labour First Minister, Jack McConnell in September 2006. He complained that Whitehall officials normally ignore Scottish views. Whitehall, he said, 'appeared to be under the impression that their policy views and objectives were representative of the entire UK, rather than those of England'[13]. This was particularly unfortunate in matters of fishing policy. Scotland had more than 70 per cent of the UK fishing fleet and 90 per cent of its fish farming. British representatives in Brussels have constantly sacrificed the interests of Scottish fishing for the sake of some other advantage. An industry which is important to Scotland, but not to anything like the same extent to England, has been devastated in consequence.

Scottish independence does not mean separation, as the Labour Party frequently alleges. Gordon Brown, for example, in his speech to the Scottish Labour Party conference on 28 March 2008 said: 'This is an interdependent world. What sense would it make within these islands to separate Scotland from the rest of Britain and make it more difficult to travel and trade? The Union enhances the influence of Scottish people and ideas'[14]. Brown is living in the past when the world was dominated by the empires and the multi-national states. Almost all of them have now dissolved into their component parts. Because of this, and the increased role of international organisations, the world has become much more interdependent.

Scotland can only benefit from it when we join the modern world by recovering independence.

An independent Scotland would remain a member of the European Union and a valuable one because of our skilled population and resources including oil and fish. Our freedom of movement and trade is not confined to Britain, as Brown seems to suggest, but includes the whole area of the European Union and much of the rest of the world. Scotland can become a full and active participant in the new interdependent world as a member state of the EU and the UN. Another Labour Minister, Des Browne, has the habit of attaching the adjective 'parochial' to the aspirations of the SNP Government whenever he mentions it, as he did at the same conference[15]. For centuries the Scots have been enthusiastic cosmopolitans. The parochial are those who want to deny us our right to participate in the world at large.

Opponents of Scottish independence have suggested that Scotland would not automatically remain a member of the European Union when it achieves independence, and would have to apply as a new applicant. There are no grounds in European legislation for this opinion. Several senior authorities have confirmed this. For instance, Emile Noel, a former Secretary General of the European Commission, said:

> There is no precedent and no provision for the expulsion of a member state, therefore Scottish independence would create two new member states out of one. They would have equal status with each other and with the other member states.
>
> The remainder of the United Kingdom would not be in a more powerful position than Scotland. ... Anyone attacking the claim in respect of one country is attacking it in respect of the other. It s not possible to divide the cases[16].

Both countries would have to negotiate such matters as their voting strength in the Council and number of members in the

European Parliament. Since there would be no need for a new application, there would be no risk of a suspension of membership or of a veto.

The Psychological Damage Inflicted by the Union

It is not in economic matters alone that Scotland suffers from the Union. The psychological consequences in the loss of self-knowledge and self–confidence is even more damaging. That this can be said of the Scots of all peoples is extraordinary. For centuries before the Union Scotland played an active and constructive part in European affairs. Scots studied and taught in European universities. Between its foundation and the Reformation 17 or 18 of the Rectors of the University of Paris were Scots[17]. In the 17th century George Buchanan was celebrated all over Europe as the best poet in Latin since classical times. Several Scots served European governments as ministers and diplomats, a rare act of confidence in foreigners. Scots were in demand to assist in the development of many countries. Lord Macaulay attributed this to the quality of Scottish education, and he was of course speaking of Scottish education in the 16th and 17th centuries:

> It began to be evident that the common people of Scotland were superior in intelligence to the common people of any country in Europe... Scotland made good progress in all that constitutes civilisation... This wonderful change is to be attributed, not indeed solely, but principally to the national system of education[18].

Following the discovery of America and the rest of the world Scots made an important contribution to the development of many countries overseas, particularly, but not confined to, North America and the Empire.

Inside Scotland itself our history has been one of remarkable achievement. For three centuries we successfully survived attacks by our larger and more powerful neighbour. In the course of this we evolved ideas of equality and representative government. Many Americans regard the Declaration of Arbroath of 1320 as the source from which their own constitution derives. The Church of Scotland created a democratic structure for the control of its affairs centuries before any parliament did the same. In ideas, scientific discovery, exploration, literature and the arts Scotland has a remarkable record. In the words of the American, Harold Orel in his book on Scotland, 'no nation of its size has contributed as much to world culture'[19]. And, of course, another American, Arthur Herman, in his book, *The Scottish Enlightenment: The Scots' Invention of the Modern World* concluded : 'As the first modern nation and culture, the Sots have by and large made the world a better place'[20].

The obvious question is how can the people of such a country possibly lack self-confidence? The immediate answer is that a great many Scots, probably the majority, know virtually nothing about the history and literature of their own country. This is, of course, shocking and disgraceful, especially in a country with a past of such rich achievement as Scotland. As the English historian, J. A. Froude said: 'No nation in Europe can look back with more just pride on their past than the Scots, and no young Scot ought to grow up in ignorance of what that past has been'[21]. But that is precisely what has happened. For several generations our schools have largely ignored our own history and literature, and so have the broadcasters, to an extent probably unique in the developed world. Our children have been given the impression that they are growing up in a backward and benighted place which has never accomplished anything of importance. It is not surprising that many want to leave as soon as they can.

This has been a consequence, slowly but probably inevitably, of the Union of 1707, a process which is the subject of Michael Hechter's book, *Internal Colonialism*, published in 1975. He concludes that in order to assert authority the centre 'must disparage the indigenous culture of peripheral groups'. It does this by claiming its own culture is 'vastly superior' for the realisation of universal ends. This 'process of anglicisation' is carried through 'not only by government fiat, but through the voluntary assimilation of peripheral elites'[22]. That such a process has been carried through and is still in action is, I think undeniable; but it has probably been more unconscious than deliberate. It is the natural consequence of a Union in which one partner is so much larger and wealthier than the other and has all the instruments of power in its control.

This process has been helped too by the self-confidence of the English and their assumption that they enjoy a natural superiority over the rest of us. The 'peripheral elite', as Hechter calls it, from Scotland, who sought royal patronage, or political or worldly success in London, had to play by these rules. Schools in Scotland began to feel obliged to assist in this process. The bairns could only succeed in the world if they learnt to speak English. The consequences of this gradually spread through Scotland. In Derrick McClure's words, 'In the 19th century, even the name and identity of Scotland, and everything that made it distinctively Scottish, became suspect as the Scots came to regard English mores, as the English themselves regarded them – as the natural models for the rest of the world'[23].

The undermining of Scottish self-confidence began effectively in the 19th century because that was when the British Empire dominated Scottish life. Many Scots made brilliant careers in its administration and millions emigrated to it. Others opened up new territories through exploration. Scottish regiments in a more controversial role were active in its expansion and security. Scottish industry built a major part of the ships and railway locomotives which served it. Other Scottish industries imported raw materials from it and exported their products to it. All of this was, as Linda Colley has said, 'a British imperium... The English and the foreign are still all too inclined today to refer to the island of Great Britain as 'England'. But at no time have they ever referred to an *English* empire'[24]. Since this institution had become so important in the life of Scotland and since Scotland was a partner in it only because of the Union, there was pressure towards Scottish opinion taking a favourable view of the Union itself.

Distortions in Unionist Propaganda

It was in this atmosphere that two theories about the Union began to be accepted which place it in a favourable light, but which are in fact false. They have survived to the present and probably colour the attitude of many people to the Union and therefore to Scottish independence. They have become so thoroughly established that even reputable academics still to this day repeat them as if they were undeniable truths. Since they have survived so long and with so much effect, it is, I think, appropriate to explain them in some detail.

The first of these is a version of the origin of the Union. It is said that the failure of the Darien scheme imposed such a loss on Scotland that the Scottish Parliament had to seek the help of the English. In response the English Government proposed negotiations. These led to a Treaty which was freely negotiated and ratified by the Scottish Parliament. It included the full compensation by the British Government of the losses of the Darien investors and access to Scottish traders to the English colonial markets. The two countries were merged into one, called Great Britain, with a combined Parliament. Scotland prospered accordingly.

It all sounds too good to be true, and that is what it is. All of these statements are the precise opposite of the truth. After Darien the Scottish Parliament did not seek English help; but in the sessions of 1703 and 1704 voted repeatedly for the recovery of Scottish independence and the restoration of a separate Scottish monarchy. Godolphin, the leading minister in the English Government, in a letter to Seafield, the Scottish Chancellor, threatened war. The English Parliament then passed an Act proposing negotiations, but also threatening stringent economic sanctions if the Scots did not accept the same succession to the throne as England by 25 December 1705. When the Scottish Parliament discussed the appointment of commissioners for negotiations in London, Hamilton (almost certainly because of bribery) contrived a decision that this should be left to the Queen. This meant that both teams of negotiators were appointed by the English Government and a genuine and free negotiation was therefore impossible.

The Treaty of Union which emerged provided for the abolition of the Scottish Parliament, and for Scottish access to trade with the English colonies. It also imposed heavy financial burdens on Scotland in the form of a share in liability for the English National Debt and the imposition of English excise duties. In compensation for these, and to repay the losses of the Scottish investors in Darien, a sum of money, called the Equivalent, was to be paid to Scotland. In fact, this sum was inadequate to cover all its purposes and even that amount was never paid in full. In a debate which lasted from October 1706 to January 1707 the Scottish Parliament approved the Treaty. This was the same Parliament with the same members who had voted repeatedly in favour of Scottish independence. There is little room for doubt that they yielded to bribery and the threat of invasion. The population at large protested against the Union by demonstrations in the streets and a flood of addresses, all against and not one in favour. The Parliament, like all others at that time, was completely unrepresentative, consisting only of lords, lairds and members provided by the oligarchies that controlled the burghs.

The immediate effect of the Treaty was to depress the Scottish economy for several decades. Adam Smith in a letter in 1760 explained the reasons:

> The immediate effect of it was to hurt the interest of every single order of men in the country... Even the merchants seemed to suffer at first. The trade to the Plantations was, indeed, opened to them. But that was a trade which they knew nothing about; the trade they were acquainted with, that to France, Holland and the Baltic, was laid under new embarrassments which almost totally annihilated the two first and most important

> branches... No wonder if at that time all orders of men conspired in cursing a measure so hurtful to their immediate interest.[25]

The other long-enduring myth is the allegation, often repeated even by serious historians of literature, that Walter Scott was an enthusiast for the Union. In the present climate, his views on such a matter may seem unimportant; but his significance in his own lifetime and for at least a century afterwards was as dominant as his monument in Edinburgh suggests. He was regarded not only as one of the greatest Scottish writers but as a great Scottish patriot who had restored the self-confidence of the Scottish people and their awareness of their own history. When Scott died in 1832 Henry Cockburn said of him in his Journal: 'Scotland never owed so much to one man'[26]. Harold Macmillan in an address to the Edinburgh Sir Walter Scott Club said: 'For Scotland, he achieved two great ends. He made her people and her history known in every part of the civilised world. In addition he made Scotland known to herself'[27].

Clearly if such a man approved of the Union, who could be against it? But again, the facts are quite different. Throughout his life Scott was deeply worried that the effect of the Union would be to destroy the distinctive character of Scotland. Lockhart in his *Life of Scott* describes an episode in 1806 when Scott had been at a meeting in the Faculty of Advocates at which changes in legal procedure were discussed. As he walked down the Mound afterwards with some of his fellow advocates, Francis Jeffrey congratulated Scott on his eloquence and energy in opposing the changes and treated the matter playfully. Lockhart continues:

> But his feelings had been moved to an extent far beyond their apprehension: he exclaimed: 'No, No 'tis no laughing matter; little by little, whatever your wishes may be, you will destroy and undermine, until nothing that makes Scotland Scotland shall remain.'
>
> And so saying, he turned round to conceal his

> agitation – but not until Mr Jeffrey saw tears gushing down his cheek – resting his head until he recovered himself on the wall of the Mound[28].

In his *Tales of a Grandfather*, a history of Scotland for children, Scott wrote a frank account of the way in which England had achieved the Union. He concluded:

> Men of whom a majority had thus been bought and sold, forfeited every right to interfere in the terms which England insisted upon... but despised by the English, and detested by their own country, ... had no alternative left save that of fulfilling the unworthy bargain they had made... a total surrender of their independence, by their false and corrupted statesmen into the hand of their proud and powerful rival[29].

Angus Calder has a point when he says that it was possible in the late 18th century even for Walter Scott to tolerate the Union because 'so far, it had not entailed any serious loss of Scottish distinctiveness imposed by England'[30]. Earlier in the century the British Parliament had seriously intervened in Scottish affairs by passing an Act providing for the appointment of ministers in the Church of Scotland by landowners and not by election by the congregation. Eventually this led to the division of the Church by the Disruption of 1843. In the middle of the 18th century the British Government defeated, with Scottish participation, the Jacobite rising and then proceeded to destroy the established form of Highland society. Even so, it is true that the British Government for the rest of the century, having reduced Scotland to political impotence, generally left it to find its own way with its remaining institutions.

This began to change early in the 19th century to the alarm of Walter Scott. He seized the opportunity presented by the Government's proposal in 1826 of an Act to abolish the right of Scottish banks to issue their own bank notes He said in a letter to his close associate, John Ballantyne: 'I shall sleep quieter in my grave for having so fair an opportunity of speaking my mind'[31]. This he did in three strongly worded essays in an Edinburgh newspaper which were subsequently published as a pamphlet, *The Letters of Malachi Malagrowther on the Proposed Change of Currency.* They are the first manifesto of modern Scottish nationalism.

Scotland, he said, 'was left from the year 1750 under the guardianship of her own institutions, to find her silent way to national wealth and consequence'. This she had achieved with such success that she 'has increased her prosperity in a ratio more than five times greater than that of her more fortunate and richer sister. She is now worth the attention of the learned faculty, and God knows she has had plenty of it... A spirit of proselytism has of late shown itself in England for extending the benefits of their system, in all its strengths and weaknesses, to a country, which has hitherto flourishing and contented under its own. They adopted the conclusion, that all English enactments are right; but the system of municipal law in Scotland is not English, therefore it is wrong... There has been in England a gradual and progressive system of assuming the management of affairs entirely and exclusively proper to Scotland, as if we were totally unworthy of having the management of our own concerns. All must centre in London... Good Heaven, sir! To what are we fallen? – or rather, what are we esteemed by the English? Wretched drivellers, incapable of understanding our own affairs; or greedy peculators, unfit to be trusted? On what ground are we considered either the one or the other?... For God's sake, sir, let us remain as Nature made us. Englishmen, Irishmen and Scotchmen, with something like the impress of our several countries upon each!... The Scottish Members of Parliament should therefore lose no time – not an instant – in uniting together in their national character of the Representatives of Scotland'[32].

Scott's indignation, and his worry for the future, were clearly aroused both by English intervention in Scottish affairs and by the effect that this was likely to have on the attitudes of the people. The apparent English assumption that the Scots could not be trusted to deal with their own problems was humiliating. Were we too stupid, incompetent or dishonest? Over time this was a process that could undermine Scottish self-confidence. The acceptance for years of the two obvious distortions of the facts, which I have described, suggests that this is what in fact happened.

Inevitably the publication of the *Malachi Letters* created an immediate reaction. Petitions against the proposed law on banknotes flooded into Parliament from all parts of Scotland and the proposed legislation was soon withdrawn. Hugh MacDiarmid has said that Scott's argument 'leads naturally on to the separatist position', meaning Scottish independence[33]. But it was a very slow process. Increasingly in the 19th century attention concentrated on the Empire and not on Scotland itself. The *Malachi Letters* themselves, although the most pungent and outspoken of all Scott's works, became the least well known. It was a virtual censorship.

The Consequences of the Empire

In the course of the 19th century the Empire greatly stimulated the Scottish economy as a source of raw materials and a market for exports. Many Scots made a fortune in trade. Others had brilliant careers in the administration, development and defence of the Empire, which became unmistakably a British, and not only an English, enterprise. All of this was a consequence of the Union which, for that reason, became much more acceptable to Scottish opinion, almost beyond criticism.

At the same time, concentration on the Empire had disadvantages. People flooded from the countryside to the towns in search of employment. Scotland had no authority to deal with the social problems which followed from over-crowding, poor housing, unemployment and poverty. Over two million Scots emigrated between 1815 and 1939. We have still found no solution to the consequences of all of this.

The Empire dissolved rapidly after the 1939–45 War as the former colonies became independent. Paradoxically, Wales and Scotland, which in a sense are the oldest colonies, are still for most purposes under the control of the Westminster Parliament in which their MPs are a small minority. If the Empire benefited Scotland in the days of the Empire, is there any case for it when the Empire no longer exists?

Resurgence

Towards the end of the 19th century there was a resurgence in both cultural and political self-confidence. There is always a close relationship between them. In the 1880s the Scottish Home Rule Association was formed and the conference of the Scottish Liberal Party adopted for the first time the policy of Home Rule for Scotland; the office of Secretary of State for Scotland was restored; the Scottish National Portrait Gallery, the Scottish Text Society and the Scottish History Society were founded. R. L. Stevenson wrote *Kidnapped* and *The Master of Ballantrae*; William McTaggart was painting some of his finest pictures; Greig and Duncan collected 3,500 folk songs in Aberdeenshire alone. By 1895, Patrick Geddes was able to write in his periodical *Evergreen* of a Scots Renaissance, long before the term was applied to the movement associated with Hugh MacDiarmid. Geddes himself was a leader in this revival, devoted to the cause of escaping from 'the intellectual thraldom of London' and restoring the old sympathies between Scotland and continental Europe[34]. In 1889 the first of a series of Home Rule for Scotland Bills were presented to the House of Commons, They made steady progress until they were interrupted by the First World War.

This war inflicted great damage on Scotland which suffered a disproportionate rate of casualties. Some people had doubts about the possibility of a Scottish recovery. There is, for instance, a well-known passage at the end of Lewis Grassic Gibbon's novel, *Sunset Song*, where he speaks of four of his characters, farm workers from the Mearns, who were killed in France:

> With them we may say there died a thing older than themselves, these were the Last of the Peasants, the last

> of the Old Scots folk. A new generation comes up that will know them not, except as a memory in a song.
>
> ... It was the old Scotland that perished then, and we may believe that never again will the old speech and the old songs, the old curses and the old benedictions, rise but with alien effort to our lips[35].

In 1935 Edwin Muir made a tour through Scotland which he described in his book, *Scottish Journey*. He drew the conclusion from the experience that Scotland 'is now falling to pieces, for there is no visible and effective power to hold it together'[36]. Several other writers reached a similar conclusion.

But there were already other forces at work determined to prevent such a disaster. The Scottish National Party, devoted to the recovery of Scottish independence was founded in 1931. At about the same time many other organisations were established to encourage aspects of Scottish culture. They included the Scottish National Trust in 1932 to safeguard important Scottish buildings and countryside, and the Saltire Society in 1936, 'to encourage everything that might improve the quality of life in Scotland and restore the country to its proper place as a creative force in European civilisation'[37]. Other organisations were devoted to the Gaelic and Scots languages, literature and traditional music. At the same time, Hugh MacDiarmid stimulated both a literary and a political revival. The campaign to recover the Scottish Parliament, which began in the previous century, eventually succeeded with a decisive referendum in 1997. This was for a Parliament with strictly limited powers. The SNP campaigned for it because they thought it a step in the right direction, and Labour for the opposite reason that they hoped that it would discourage anything more ambitious.

The long period of subservience to the capital of another country with very different traditions and ideas from our own has inevitably had demoralising and debilitating consequences. Eric Linklater said in his book, *The Lion and The Unicorn:*

> People degenerate when they lose control of their own affairs, and, as a corollary, resumption of control may

> induce regeneration. To any nation the essential vitamin is responsibility.
>
> By reason of its association with England, Scotland became insular. Its political frontier was broken down and its mind was walled up. Geographical or political enlargement, beyond certain limits, is nearly always accompanied by intellectual shrinkage[38].

I have already mentioned the adverse effects on our self-confidence of broadcasting controlled by London and of a curriculum in many schools which largely ignores our own history and literature and does its best to eradicate the Scots language. Broadcasting is probably the more damaging. It is a life-long influence after all and is probably the major one for most people. There are some good programmes but the vast majority ignore Scotland and take no account of our experiences and ideas. For this reason, the distinguished historian, Geoffrey Barrow, said that our failure to establish a Scottish organisation for public sector broadcasting was the greatest cultural disaster which Scotland suffered in the 20th century[39]. A senior official of the BBC said that it is the glue which held the Union together. It was presumably for this reason that when Labour drew up the Act to establish the devolved Scottish Parliament they made it responsible for cultural policy, but kept control of broadcasting, the most potent means of cultural expression, firmly in the hands of Westminster.

We can see the consequences of these influences in a report published in the Spring of 2008. This was the work of the Glasgow Centre for Population Health and NHS Health Scotland[40]. They found that life expectancy was shorter in the West of Scotland than in the most deprived areas of Eastern Europe and was improving more slowly than anywhere else. This has been attributed to low self-esteem, pessimism and lack of ambition, attitudes which are particularly acute in the West probably because of the decline in traditional industries. There was a time when Glasgow built a large proportion of the world's steam ships and railway locomotives and steel and coal mining were flourishing industries in the West of Scotland. Ship building is a shadow of its former self and the rest have virtually disappeared. The drift of ownership and control to the south has added to the decline. Such a major and long neglected problem demands the attention of a Scottish Government with the powers of independence.

We also need to improve the quality of our intellectual response to our problems. Broadcasting can help, but in both radio and television it has sharply deteriorated in recent years. News programmes often concentrate, not on important events, especially if they are in other countries, but on crime, the pointless activities of so-called celebrities and sport. There are very few programmes which show intelligence and an attempt to deal seriously with serious subjects. Perhaps this is a reflection of the current taste of the London audience. I am optimistic enough to think that we shall do much better in Scotland when we have our own public service broadcasting organisation. I hope that it would reflect our traditional enthusiasm for education, the democratic intellect, philosophical thought, scientific discovery and international relations. It is significant that the best BBC television programme on developments in Europe is the one in Gaelic.

Independence will not only make Scotland more prosperous and self-confident, but it will also help us to make a contribution, as in the past, to the development of other countries, in political and social ideas and in literature and the arts. Scotland will be a useful member of the European Union and the United Nations. Independence will also greatly improve our relations with England by removing the grievances caused by the Union and increased by Devolution. It is, for example, unacceptable that Members of the Westminster Parliament for Scottish constituencies can vote on matters affecting only England. Independent Scotland will be able to speak for its own interests in the Councils of Europe. On issues where we agree, which will be most of them, we shall have a stronger influence as two members than we have at present as one. As two independent neighbours, Scotland and England will have a close and friendly relationship when we are free from the irritations and complications of a Union which no longer has a useful purpose for either of us.

The experience of an SNP Government devoted to the radical improvement of conditions in Scotland has transformed the political situation. The advantages of independence are so great and so obvious that it cannot be long before we demand it in a referendum. At my age, I only hope that I live long enough to see it.

Notes

1 E. F. Schumacher, *Small is Beautiful,* (London, 1974) Reprint of 1977, pp. 52–3

2 *Key Facts and Figures about Europe and the European Union,* (Luxembourg, 2007. Office for Official Publications of the European Union)

3 David Hume, *Selected Essays,* ed. Stephen Copley and Andrew Edgar, (Oxford, 1993) p. 311

4 Adam Ferguson, *An Essay on the History of Civil Society,* 1767, ed. Duncan Forbes. (Edinburgh, 1966) p. 59

5 As 1, p. 53

6 Johan P. Olsen in *The Future of the Nation State* ed. Sverker Gustavsson and Leif Lewin, (London 1996) pp. 274–5

7 Poul Schluter, in *Analysis* on BBC Radio 4, 19 September 1991

8 Garret Fitzgerald in *Scotland on Sunday,* 30 April 1989

9 Mary Robinson in *The Scotsman,* 29 June 1992

10 Hume Brown, *The Union of 1707.* (Glasgow, 1907) p. 4

11 Iain Banks in *Edinburgh Evening News,* 15 March 2008

12 *The Herald,* 29 December 2005 and 30 January 2006

13 *The Herald,* 21 January 2007

14 *The Scotsman,* 30 March 2008

15 *The Scotsman,* 31 March 2008

16 Emile Noel in *Scotland on Sunday,* 5 March 1989 and *The Scotsman,* 12 June 1989

17 Alexander Broadie, *The Tradition of Scotish Philosophy* (Edinburgh, 1990) p. 3

18 T. B. Macaulay, *History of England* (London, 1858) Vol. IV. pp. 782–3

19 Harold Orel, *The Scottish World: History and Culture of Scotland* (London, 1981) p. 12

20 Arthur Herman, op. cit. (London, 1981) p. 12

21 J. A. Froude quoted by Prof. Gordon Donaldson in his Inaugural Lecture in the University of Edinburgh, 1964

22 Michael Hechter, op. cit. (London, 1973) pp. 64, 73, 80

23 J. Derrick McClure in *Why Scots Matters* (4th edition, Edinburgh, 2008)

24 Linda Colley in *Britons: Forging the Nation, 1707–1837* (Yale, 1992) p. 130

25 Adam Smith, *Correspondence,* ed. E. C. Mosner and I. C. Ross. (Glasgow, 1994) p. 68

26 Henry Cockburn, *Journal. 1831–54.* (Edition of 1874, Edinburgh) Vol I p. 37

27 Harold Macmillan in *Talking About Scott*, ed. Ian Campbell and Peter Garside, (Edinburgh, 1994) p. 49

28 J. G. Lockhart, *Memoirs of Sir Walter Scott*, (Edition of 1900, London) Vol I, p. 460

29 Sir Walter Scott, *Tales of a Grandfather*, (Edition of 1889, Edinburgh) p. 770

30 Angus Calder, *Revolving Culture,* (London and New York, 1994) p. 69

31 Sir Walter Scott, *Letters,* ed. by H. J. C. Grierson., (London, 1935) Vol IX, p. 437

32 Sir Walter Scott, *The Letters of Malachi Malagrowther*, ed. by P. H. Scott, (Edinburgh, 1981) pp 9–10, 136–137, 143, 72

33 Hugh MacDiarmid, *Lucky Poet.* (London, 1943) p. 203

34 Patrick Geddes quoted in Philip Mairet, *Pioneer of Sociology: The Life and Letters of Patrick Geddes, (*London, 1957) p. 68

35 Lewis Grassic Gibbon, *Sunset Song*, (in the Trilogy Edition, *A Scots* Quair, London, 1971) p. 193

36 Edwin Muir, *Scottish Journey*, (Edition of 1979, Edinburgh) p. 25

37 Saltire Society Syllabus 2007–8

38 Eric Linklater, *The Lion and the Unicorn*, (London, 1935) pp. 26, 130

39 Geoffrey Barrow in a lecture to the Saltire Society

40 *Sunday Herald,* 6 April 2008 and BBC Newsnight Scotland, 7 April 2008

CHAPTER 3

The Fish, the Ferry and the Black Crude Reality

Neil Kay

THE 1973 PLAY *The Cheviot, the Stag and the Black, Black Oil* by John McGrath was a phenomenon that was very much of its time. It mixed rising nationalist sentiment and a growing consciousness of the prospects that oil could hold for economic independence with what was left over from the '60s desire for radical reform. At least it did for me, just about on my way to my first job as a professional economist, with my rising nationalist sentiment and my residual radicalism left over from a '60s student lifestyle.

That play reflected the politics of socialism, itself a distinguished and well established tradition in Scotland, but it also reflected the politics of grievance, equally well established, but much less distinguished. After the sound and fury of the performance it left the question; 'well... what are you going to do about it?'

I also remember from the following year the American reporter from *Time* magazine who had been touring Scotland in a taxi looking for stories on 'resurgent nationalism', and who was now homing in on Stirling University as a well known hotbed of rabid revolutionaries. But he found 'no demonstrations, no underground armies of the night, no threats of violence in the air'[1], which, while reassuring for the cause of stable governance, did not make for great copy. I had seen McGrath's play the previous year, and while I cannot remember whether my answer was influenced by that experience, I do remember the reporter pressing us hard on why we did not want to take government by storm. As *Time* magazine reported in April 1974:

> 'You can't live day to day with your own rage,' says Neil Kay, 25, a graduate student in economics at Stirling University and a Nationalist activist. 'If we're going to do anything, we are going to do it by rational and reasonable methods.'[2]

In my defence, I was in the process of transmuting to nationalism after a long sojourn in the Liberal Party, and had just spent seven years studying economics at undergraduate and post-graduate level. If by then you had not accepted the basic economic premise that all individuals are rational decision-makers, you would have quickly found out you had no future in the economics profession. But 'Independence by all rational and reasonable methods' does not a stirring call to action make, especially when uttered in the shade of the Wallace Monument, just a few miles from Bannockburn.

Now 34 years on, after numerous encounters with politicians, but particularly with civil servants (for whom Dante might reasonably have dedicated a special Circle), I am not so convinced now as I was then that rational reasonable argument may be sufficient. I am also less convinced than I was then that some occasional rage (non-violent, properly channelled) would necessarily be a bad thing.

If my views have evolved over the years, then much the same could be said of economics. Economics today has largely recognised and even tentatively embraced concepts such as irrationality, ignorance and other aspects reflecting the contrariness and fallibility of human nature. At the same time, I cannot completely forswear the default working premise that I have inherited down the years as an economist which I might express now as: when all else fails, fall back on rational, reasonable argument.

After several decades of arguments and debates on the economics of Scottish independence with sceptics, I find that issues can be sharpened and clarified by ignoring the Scottish case to begin with and asking the sceptic just two questions. Question (a) do you believe that separate countries should exist? If the sceptic answers in the negative, there is no point in proceeding any further. But if, as most do, they answer in the positive (albeit reluctantly in some cases) then you proceed to the second question. Question (b) what principles should determine the boundaries of countries?

At that point you can have a useful discussion about the role of shared or distinctive legal, political, historical, cultural institutions in creating sensible principles for setting the boundaries of nations, always subject to the popular will, while citing cases to illustrate the point. At some stage the sceptic will usually sense which way the wind is blowing as far as the case for Scottish independence is concerned. What I find is that many will attempt to pre-empt this by arguing that even if there was a case for Scottish independence, actually getting there would be too painful or too costly. In short, they will implicitly argue that the temporary process and costs of transition would trump any subsequent long term gains that could be achieved under independence itself.

One of the most quoted phrases in economics is John Maynard Keynes's: 'In the long run we are all dead'[3]. Some sceptics, particularly those with a background in economics, are prone to quote Keynes at this point as an effective rebuttal of the case for the long term benefits of an independent Scotland. Concentrate on the here and now, they will argue, avoid the costs and distraction of a painful separation and an uncertain future.

What is less well known than Keynes's aphorism is the sentence that preceded it; 'Long run is a misleading guide to current affairs'[4]. That is the context in which he was arguing and it is as true today as it was in 1923. The long term forecasts for the global economy in 10 years time are not much help to the Monetary Policy Committee when it has to set interest rates today. But that does not mean that sensible action today cannot be taken with a view to influencing events well beyond the short term horizon, otherwise none of us would take out a 20-year mortgage, buy insurance, or even educate our children. Keynes himself was very much aware of the interconnectedness between the present and the future, as would be expected from one who essayed on 'economic possibilities for our grandchildren'[5]. The problem with Keynes' aphorism regarding mortality and the long run is that when it is quoted out of context it can mesh well with, and help justify, political short-termism and natural instincts towards small 'c' conservatism, apathy, and inertia.

We take here as given that the current boundaries of Scotland would represent a sensible basis around which to constitute an independent country; the legal, political, historical, cultural justification for this has been made many times before, and will be made many times again, leaving the only issue to be settled that of the popular will. What I want to concentrate on is the question of alternatives, and to short cut the discussion I will focus on what are the only two likely alternatives, the status quo (albeit with some further minor devolution of powers) and independence within Europe. Even moderate reform of the status quo would quickly come up against such issues as the Barnett Formula[6], the West Lothian Question[7], fiscal autonomy, and the issue of oil funds. It is difficult to conceive of any package of constitutional reforms that could deliver a stable outcome (holding measures such as the Calman Commission[8] notwithstanding), bearing in mind that they would have to achieve a political consensus on both sides of the border. As for independence, it is also assumed that this means independence within the EC, there being little evidence of political or popular will for any alternative to Community membership.

A Union Dividend?

Is there a 'Union Dividend' for Scotland from continuing with the UK? In 2006, the then First Minister Jack McConnell said in a speech;

> 'We all benefit from a Union dividend and all that it secures – the free movement of citizens, the increase in

> trade and opportunities for our businesses and the sharing of values and aspirations'[9].

But is that it? After 300 years, one would hope for a little more substance in defence of the Union. The first two items on this very short list (free movement of citizens, increase in trade and opportunities for business) are now delivered as a matter of statutory obligation and rote though membership of a wider union within Europe, rendering UK union membership redundant in these respects. Probing these items reveals them to be little more than versions of the 'access to Empire markets' which passed their sell-by date many years ago.

Even when it might have had arguable validity, the 'access to Empire' argument was actually a form of political protection racket to the effect that you would be given reason to be sorry if you did not join our Empire-ya-bas gang. It is irrelevant today in the context of a globalised market and a European Union.

As for the idea that maintenance of the Union is necessary for 'sharing of values and aspirations', it is difficult to see how Irish independence has impeded healthy cross-fertilisation of ideas and cultures back and forth across the Irish sea, and it is equally difficult to see how and why that would or should happen in the case of Scottish independence.

A 'family ties' version of the 'sharing of values and aspirations' argument was recently put forward by Gordon Brown when he promoted a Fabian pamphlet[10] he co-authored with Douglas Alexander. The UK Prime Minister said the pamphlet would make the '21st century case for the Union', and that case would be built on family ties. 'When the Act of Union was signed, only 30,000 Scots had English relatives, and now the figure is 2.5 million,' Mr Brown said. 'It will seem strange to consider breaking a union when 2.5 million Scots have strong ties, family ties, with England.'[11].

But it did not seem strange to the citizenry of the United States in 1776, in their own Declaration of Independence when they declaimed: 'Nor have we been wanting in attentions to our British brethren... we have conjured [sic] them by the ties of our common kindred... They too have been deaf to the voice of justice and of consanguinity'[12].

In fact, 'family ties' do not have a very convincing or respectable track record in debates about independence, whether it is the white Rhodesians 'having demonstrated loyalty to the Crown and to their kith and kin in the United Kingdom and elsewhere', as they made clear in their Unilateral Declaration of Independence[13], to the old Soviet argument about not giving the Baltic states independence because so many Russian citizens lived there.

Indeed, a counter argument could be made that, rather than facilitating the 'sharing' of values and aspiration, the Union has led to undue and unhealthy homogenisation, with the dominant partner in this Union dictating the terms. Like many of my baby boomer generation growing up in Scotland, I was taught that if you were reasonably clever, you did languages, if you were fairly clever you did Latin, and if you were really clever you did Latin *and* Greek. I have no recollection of anyone ever telling us why that was the case, I had to work it out later for myself. In fact, a knowledge of classics was a prerequisite for an Oxbridge education, indeed Latin had been a required subject for applicants to Oxford and Cambridge until the 1960s. If you wanted an exemplar from the education sphere of the 'sharing of values and aspirations' that was part and parcel of the Union dividend, then Oxbridge was it.

Of course, Latin and Greek can be interesting and stimulating intellectual disciplines but the crucial economic notion here is that of opportunity cost, or the value of the alternatives which might have been pursued instead of the chosen activity. As with any rating or rankings system, if something is prized highly, the corollary is that other things are not so highly valued. If you were not so clever, it was made very clear to you that your future was more likely to lie with the technical and engineering subjects.

At the very time in history when Scotland should have been consolidating and building on its status as 'the World's Workshop' in Tom Devine's graphic phrase[14], we were teaching our children that the pinnacle of intellectual excellence lay in knowing the difference between ablative absolutes and subordinate relative clauses in long dead foreign languages, benchmarked as preparation for an entrance exam they would never sit, for an Oxbridge university that would not want them, and to which they would probably not wish to go even if the opportunity arose.

If one image could serve as a metaphor for Scotland's 20th century industrial decline, it would be serried ranks of redundant cranes along the Clyde and serried ranks of children in classrooms across Scotland chanting 'amo, amas, amat'. This would also serve as an endnote to one of the most remarkable stories of industrial power and influence wielded from a population base that was still less than five million by the end of its peak.

This phenomenon is described in detail by Tom Devine[15]. He narrates how Scotland advanced from a relatively low industrial base around 1830 to a position of global dominance in several key sectors in a few decades: 'coal, iron, steel, shipbuilding and engineering took off and transformed Scotland into a manufacturer for the world'[16]. At one point, Coats of Paisley controlled 80 per cent of global thread-making capacity. At the time of World War 1, Scotland had built about one-fifth of the world's shipping tonnage then in use. 'At the heart of the heavy industrial complex with its world-wide markets was the huge range of engineering specialisms in engine pumps, hydraulic equipment, railway rolling stock and a host of other products'[17].

It was not just the sheer scale of industrialisation and emergent Scottish industrial power and prestige that had been so impressive from the early 19th century onwards, it was the impetus provided by Scottish technological developments. Devine notes[18] that a primary factor in Scotland's transformation was a remarkable rate of strategic invention and innovation in metal working and ship construction, and the story of rapid technological progress added to other sectors in this rich industrial broth.

The final element in this transformation was the interdependencies and technological spillovers between industries and sectors. 'It was perhaps almost inevitable that from this great congeries of skills in precision engineering would come an interest in the application of steam propulsion to ships'[19]; 'the fortunes of shipbuilding, iron and steel became very closely linked'[20] Devine also observes that Scotland's industrial base in textiles (which actually pre-dated the first Industrial Revolution) also played an important role as a catalyst for later developments in shipbuilding[21].

What Devine, the historian, is describing is what would be described by economists as an industrial cluster[22]. Industrial clusters vary in character and significance, they may be seen at the level of a city or geographical region (Silicon Valley; Detroit – 'Motor City') or even a city district (Hollywood; City of London). What we know from the work of Michael Porter[23] and others about robust and healthy industrial clusters is that they tend to be highly geographically concentrated but internationally oriented, involve networks of firms up and down supply chains, and have strong links (competitive and co-operative) at various stages within a particular industrial sector, and between firms in related sectors. It can also involve links with institutions outside the industrial sector such as universities and other sources of innovative and technical knowledge.

All of these elements were present in the creation of Silicon Valley. You can trace back the genesis of many of the companies that were to become major world players to spinoffs from Hewlett-Packard. In turn, Hewlett-Packard was the brainchild of the eponymous students who were mentored and supported by Frederick Terman, professor of electrical engineering at Stanford University. It has been said that if Hewlett and Packard were the fathers of Silicon Valley, then their teacher Frederick Terman was the grandfather.

What is also known is that there are certain conditions which are not highly conducive to cluster formation, such as stand-alone one-off entrepreneurs, concentration at limited stages of the supply chain such as production of raw materials or serving the final consumers, and a branch factory heritage which tends not to have the in-house scientific and technical expertise in branches that help spawn spin-offs. Silicon Valley in California is a healthy industrial cluster, the same could not have been said of Silicon Glen in Scotland.

There is a limit to what a government can do to encourage cluster formation, if they have a role it is more like a midwife than a parent, and just as with babies it can take a long time for clusters to grow up – typically much longer than the length of a single parliamentary term. These days, Keynes might have said; 'in the long run we just might have a viable industrial cluster'. It does take a kind of self-denying vision for politicians – and development agencies – to take the steps now that will allow their successors to reap the rewards in the future, a kind of vision that certainly politicians are not renowned for in the absence of conditions of war or depression.

These are not radical ideas, they are well established, and indeed Porter's clusters framework was adopted as policy framework by the government's development agency Scottish Enterprise in the late '90s with a number of analysts[24] providing key insights and advice as to how the framework could be applied in a Scottish context.

Scottish Enterprise certainly knows the right things and has been doing the right things, but they are essentially a facilitator and it is the fate of a facilitator to be held responsible for failure and to find the glory for any success to be appropriated by others, perhaps years down the line. That does not mean that its performance in executing a clusters strategy has been either good or bad, what it means is that if Scottish Enterprise did not exist, something like it and its clusters policy would have to be invented. What we want to know, is how effective would such strategies be in the context of Scotland's membership of the Union. The answer to that question may be found, at least in part, by considering why one of the most remarkable industrial clusters in modern industrial history unravelled so quickly and so thoroughly. Why was Scotland's 19th century industrial hegemony usurped so comprehensively in the 20th century?

Sharing values and aspirations

A simplistic answer to the question just posed would be that it was not surprising that what went up with the growth of Empire also went down with it, and that is an answer which has some attractions particularly for those who find some aspects of Scotland's association with militaristic empire-building distasteful. Certainly there is a broad coincidence of timing and it provides for a neat explanation along with other associated facts and influences such as exhaustion of raw materials, over-dependence on heavy industry, union-management relations, emergence of new low-cost competitors, and so on

But I think that the 'decline of Empire' answer is too easy, though it does add further emphasis to the irrelevance of any modern variant on the 'access to Empire' argument for keeping the Union. If we accept that Scotland hitched a very productive ride on the back of Empire, it still does not really explain why Scotland's subsequent industrial decline from its Victorian peaks was so precipitate and emphatic. Hitching rides gets you further down the road compared to those still left thumbing a lift. By the start of the 20th century, Scotland actually had quite a diversified industrial base, it had tremendous scientific and engineering resources, not just in its industrial enterprises but in its universities, and it had a well deserved international reputation for entrepreneurship, not just earned from its home-made Victorian heritage but in markets across the world. With that start in 20th century life that most countries of equivalent size would happily have swapped their own resource endowments for, how could things have gone so badly wrong?

Paradoxically, the eventual weakening of Scotland's industrial position as part of the Union might best be illustrated by examining some of its vaunted strengths. Duncan Bannatyne is a very successful self-made Scottish entrepreneur who built up a £200m chain of health clubs, but is now perhaps best known for his panel membership of the television programme *Dragons' Den* which focuses on seeking out new entrepreneurial talent. He recently argued:

> There are some phenomenal Scottish entrepreneurs, I could name so many. There's Sir Tom Hunter, Brian Souter, Sir Tom Farmer, you could go on and on. The spirit of Scottish enterprise goes back hundreds of years. Adam Smith explained markets and free enterprise, Robert Dunlop brought us Dunlop tyres, John Logie Baird brought us TV, Alexander Bell gave us the telephone, John McAdam gave us Tarmac. It was even a Scot, William Paterson, who founded the Bank of England.[25]

As far as the historical cases are concerned, if we first remove Adam Smith (who observed and documented entrepreneurship rather than practised it himself), then the single most obvious feature joining together Dunlop, Baird, Bell, McAdam and Paterson is that they all became successful after having first left Scotland. Whether that says more about the qualities of the individuals themselves, or the economic and social context they left behind, is an open question. What can be said is that the mere act of leaving your native country and having to survive without a supportive but stifling 'ah kent yer faither' social network can often be the catalyst for entrepreneurial activity. The migrant plucked from social roots can have a stronger private need for success and face less social opprobrium for failure than had they stayed home. When I grew up in Fraserburgh my newsagent was Dyga, my first (summer) job was with Borowski the photographer and had I stayed on long enough to buy my first car it would probably have been from Shrader down the road. The unifying factor underlying these three businesses is that they were all started by enterprising Polish immigrants, servicemen who had stayed on after the end of World War 2. It is important to us that Andrew Carnegie was a Scot, but perhaps equally or even more important was his familial background as economic migrants. As far as the contemporary examples of successful entrepreneurship that Bannatyne gives are concerned, Brian Souter who founded Stagecoach, Sir Tom Farmer who founded

Kwik Fit and Sir Tom Hunter who founded Sports Division are all frequently cited (often in the same breath) as exemplifying successful self-made Scottish entrepreneurship. There is absolutely no doubt they do represent exactly that, and individually and together represent superb examples of entrepreneurial activity of the highest quality. But each of them represent thin slivers of economic activity right at the end of the supply chain where it meets the final consumer. Who designed, developed and made the coaches that Stagecoach drives, the automotive components that Kwik Fit fits, the sports shoes that Sports Division sells, and the equipment that Duncan Bannatyne's health clubs use? The relevant part of the answer to each question is that it was not Scotland. As in the Sherlock Holmes story of the dog that did not bark[26], here there are several dogs that did not bark. Successful Scottish migrant entrepreneurs are one thing, but why do their reputations and performance in Scotland's story seem to overshadow those who stayed at home? Where were they all? Selling services to the final consumer in clubs, shops and buses (and, we might add through financial and tourist services) genuinely adds value, but why has Scotland not also retained or created strong presences further back up the supply chain to root these end-activities in the high value-added stages and increase the chances of creating sustainable competitive advantage that will outlive the careers of individual entrepreneurs?

This is not in any way to belittle the achievements of the seriously impressive contemporary entrepreneurs listed by (and including) Bannatyne, but it does raise questions regarding sustainable competitive advantage. It is true that Scotland is not alone amongst Western countries in going through what has been termed de-industrialisation, with service sector industries displacing manufacturing over whole swathes of the economy. Much of that is part of a natural, inevitable and indeed positive evolutionary process. But where you find modern international competitive advantage it tends not to be embodied in hero-entrepreneur figures like Alan Sugar and Donald Trump, beloved though they may be of reality TV series on both sides of the Atlantic. Instead, international competitive advantage comes in clusters of inter-related entrepreneurial activity, and whatever might be said about the excellent qualities of Souter, Farmer, Hunter and Bannatyne, membership of, or association with, a discernable industrial cluster is not one of them. I want to be clear that I am not suggesting that Scotland's industrial decline was precipitated by an unhealthy obsession with classical declensions and conjugations, to do so would be to confuse symptoms with causes. But to the extent that the final item of the Union dividend set out above by the former First Minister is concerned, 'the sharing of values and aspirations' is not one that I regard as having, on balance having had a beneficial effect on Scotland's economic performance, and try as I might, I have never found a useful application for the fact that I know that the Latin for table is 'mensa'. The most productive thing I did in Latin was to prove deficient[27] in the area of conjugations and declensions, which resulted in my banishment to engineering. The skills I subsequently learned in engineering draughtsmanship proved unexpectedly useful some decades later when I was able draw on them in using computer graphics programmes in my own economics research[28].

Much has been written[29] about Scottish education including the influence of what I would describe as Oxbridge standards but to an economist, it all comes back to opportunity cost. Again, if you make one thing a priority, you downgrade something else, and the set of values and aspirations that have been downgraded and degraded over the last century has been Scotland's engineering and scientific heritage. If this seems philistine, the contribution that liberal arts make to social and cultural life is fully acknowledged, but they should be complementary to a healthy respect for the engineering sciences, not a substitute for them. As with most things, it is a matter of emphasis and balance, and the Union heritage here has been seriously imbalanced. I think that if Scottish values and aspirations had not been overlain and crowded out by Southern values that the name of the former Chancellor of Dundee University

(1992–2006) would be regarded by many as candidate for greatest living Scot. He is certainly one of the most remarkable Scots of all time. Amongst other work he developed beta blockers and helped revolutionise heart treatment. The commercial value of the scientific work he produced could probably buy and sell the assets of an entire Dragons' Den several times over. He was awarded the Nobel Prize for Medicine in 1988. And if you have not heard of him recently, or do not even know who he is[30], that rather makes my point.

Fish, Ferries and Black Crude Realities

So where do the fish, the ferry, and the black crude reality come into all this? In some respects, as for nationalist sentiments generally, it is grounded in personal experience, but they each are also indicative of fault lines in terms of the relations between Scotland and the rest of the UK. In the part of Scotland where I grew up, just about everybody's livelihood was directly or indirectly dependent on the fish. And where I live now, just about everybody's livelihood is directly or indirectly dependent on the ferries. Such dependency is echoed up and down the North and West coasts of Scotland. The black crude reality is of course the black crude oil that has become the dominant economic activity over much of the North-East of Scotland where I come from. None of this is surprising, much of what Scotland has become today reflects the sea, most obviously from our history as a trading nation and the undersea resources around our coasts, but also in terms of the differing influences of what were proximate cultures and economies around the Scottish coast, whether west, north or east. They also have all one thing in common. These are all significant resources in a Scottish context where many livelihoods and communities depend on them. But as far as the rest of the UK is concerned, if all the fish, the ferries and the black crude oil disappeared overnight this would have relatively little impact on UK economies and societies outwith Scotland, though the Isle of Wight might feel the same pain as Mull if the ferries disappeared, while the

Treasury would find it had a black hole where once there was black gold. As far as the fish is concerned, in 2006, just three ports of Peterhead, Lerwick and Fraserburgh accounted for 49 per cent by quantity and 36 per cent by value of all landings by UK vessels into the UK[31]. While there are other localised pockets of activity outside Scotland within the UK, in relative terms the fishing industry simply does not have the same importance in the rest of the UK as it does in Scotland. Where this matters is in terms of political agendas and priorities. Within the EC, Scottish fishing policy is a UK responsibility despite the fact that it is less relevant at that level than it is in Scotland. As far as ferries are concerned, I have given invited evidence to three different Inquiries set up by the Scottish Parliament's Transport Committees (2001, 2005 and 2008). But any pretence that Scottish ministers over the years might have wished to communicate that they were somehow in control of ferry policy (for reason of vanity, credibility or whatever) was essentially a sham. When Brussels writes about policy issues concerning CalMac or Northlink ferries, they do not write to the Scottish Transport Minister or even the First Minister. They write to the UK Foreign Minister, because that is where real power and responsibility lies. And that in turn brings us to the crude reality, the issue of the oil.

Over the last few years, evidence has been accumulating that Scotland has been performing poorly judged against international comparators (including UK) in terms of growth, levels of new business formation and sluggish productivity, including the phenomenon of declining Scottish tax revenue from various sources as share of UK tax revenue[32]. At first sight this seems puzzling; after all has not Scotland had the benefit of a tremendous windfall boost to its growth opportunities with the injections of North Sea oil into the equation in recent years? Should it not be accelerating past (at the very least) its Southern neighbour rather than appearing to be falling further behind on a number of growth-related indicators?

I looked at this issue in 2007 when as one of a panel of economists I submitted invited evidence to the Scottish Parliament's

Finance Committee as part of its Inquiry into the Scottish Executive's statistical series *Government Expenditure and Revenue in Scotland.* What I found was remarkable for a number of reasons, but particularly for one crucial and central fact. Scotland's slow growth was not puzzling in the face of the North Sea oil bonanza, on the contrary it is exactly what should have been expected for any country or region which has been blessed (or cursed) with an abundance of natural resources.

The phenomenon is called the 'Resource Curse', which, even though it has strong support from empirical evidence[33], has only become widely acknowledged in the last few years. Contrary to what might be expected, countries and regions which have an abundance of natural resources (such as oil) tend to have slower growth than countries and regions which do not possess these natural assets – there is, it appears, a 'Resource Curse'. A number of possible reasons for the Resource Curse have been suggested, but one set of particular relevance to Scotland was identified by the Harvard economists Sachs and Warner[34]. They found that the demand for basic inputs (e.g. land and labour) from the natural resource sector could drive up input costs, squeezing the profits (and crowding out) internationally traded activities such as manufacturing that compete with the natural resource sector for these same inputs

Once manufacturing has been crowded out, the brakes are put on the growth process. While the Resource Curse has been most convincingly documented at country level, recent work is now suggesting that it can hold at the level of a resource-abundant region within a developed country[35], which is of course the position that Scotland finds itself in.

As I noted in my evidence to the Finance Committee, an economist from Mars, knowing all about the Resource Curse but nothing about Scotland, would not be surprised by news of the poor performance of the Scottish economy and its contingent tax revenues following the windfall of North Sea oil.

However, that is not the end of the bad news for Scotland as part of the Union. I noted in my evidence to the Finance Committee that Scotland could be doubly cursed in the absence of specific policies framed to counter a Resource Curse, the first curse (the Resource Curse itself) during the extraction phase, the second curse that of being left competitively disadvantaged with weakened tradable sectors once the oil eventually does runs out. Solution? A thoughtful – and independent – country such as Norway sets up an oil fund to help plug the gaps and create the growth opportunities that will be needed once the oil runs out. An oil fund might not guarantee happiness but it could at least provide an insurance policy against misery. To just use the oil for current consumption is eating the seed corn. But the chances of Scotland being able to negotiate its own oil fund within the Union (which even states or provinces like Alaska and Alberta have been able to do) is politically improbable given growing popular opinion outside Scotland that it is already overcompensated for through the Barnett Formula.

In some respects the arguments about the Resource Curse seem to have similarities with arguments that Scotland's public sector spending and employment have crowded out private sector activity. In fact, the crowding out argument is more about the performance of the economy, while the Resource Curse argument is about the structure of the economy. No matter how the economy is governed, we will still need police, firemen, doctors and nurses. After that, questions revolve around how well such services are organised and managed. And as far as wealth creation is concerned, a good teacher can have a long term, permanent and economy-wide effect that can outstrip many an entrepreneur, as the example of Frederick Terman demonstrates spectacularly.

Conclusions

If we did not already have a Union, few today would suggest forming it. In terms of fit between the institutions, traditions, economies, and cultures of the two countries it makes about as much sense as a Sweden/Denmark amalgamation or a France/Netherlands merger. So why does it still persist? A shrewd political observer once wrote a treatise on how to obtain and keep political power. In it he noted:

> ...there is nothing more difficult to take in hand, more perilous to conduct, or more uncertain in its success, than to take the lead in the introduction of a new order of things. Because the innovator has for enemies all those who have done well under the old conditions, and lukewarm defenders in those who may do well under the new. This coolness arises partly from fear of the opponents, who have the laws on their side, and partly from the incredulity of men, who do not readily believe in new things until they have had a long experience of them. Thus it happens that whenever those who are hostile have the opportunity to attack they do it like partisans, whilst the others defend lukewarmly.[36]

For 'the innovator' in the above quote read 'independence'. Fear, fostering of doubt and sense of inferiority, dark warnings not to risk what we have, short-termism, advocacy of the status quo – the defenders of the Union may not all have read Machiavelli's *The Prince*, but many of them behave as if they have. It is easier to scaremonger about things that exist than to guarantee what might be. But if we just exist, and simply ignore what might be, events will shape us when it is we who should be shaping events. There must be a more optimistic future for Scotland than that.

We need to drive further back up the supply chain because that is where the value is ultimately generated, more towards what Casson calls high level entrepreneurship involving major technological innovation, which he distinguishes from entrepreneurship based on market trading or shopkeeping[37]. Is the Union the best vehicle to pursue such an effort? Judging by the evidence, I would say not. Much of Scotland's innovative potential has been hollowed out over the years and if there was one crucial, defining error that could be said to be at the root of Scottish industrial twentieth century decline, it was the

Union 'dividend' of believing that 'technical' subjects were automatically and necessarily intellectually inferior to more 'academic' subjects such as the classics. To think we were all taught such utter nonsense! Try telling that to the engineers of Silicon Valley or the graduates of India's technical institutes. If America had never won its independence, the equivalent of Frederick Terman teaching in the equivalent of Stanford University would probably have been a professor of classics, while the equivalents of Hewlett and Packard could well have finished up teaching Latin and Greek at some obscure Midwestern finishing school for the sons and daughters of ranching gentlefolk.

Now, 34 years on, there are some striking similarities, but some differences, from the time that reporter interviewed that young economics student about the imminence of independence. There is again strong interest in Scottish independence, Labour is both in power and in trouble at UK level, oil is back on the agenda with a vengeance, and there is a resurgent SNP.

Differences include the fact that we have, of course, the re-creation of the Scottish Parliament which, despite some prognostications, has failed to kill Scottish independence stone dead. As far as the oil is concerned, the difference now is to be found in the basic economic lesson that when something becomes scarcer, it becomes more valuable. There may be less oil in the ground in future years, but what there is will be worth more. But the Resource Curse and the follow on consequences mean Scotland will be doubly cursed if we stay part of the Union and the North Sea continues to be treated as the Treasury's piggy bank.

Despite all that has been said here, there are grounds for hope. Scottish Enterprise's priority industries of life sciences, energy, financial markets, electronics markets are particularly suited to a clusters perspective and even the other more traditional priority industries of tourism, food and drink are ones in which Scotland has a comparative advantage. But promoting these in a Union context in many respects goes against the grain of a governance culture and philosophy which can prize a liberal arts education more highly than an engineering background. We need to get back to where we came from, which is a respect for the continuity of hands-on technical excellence and scientific brilliance that runs all the way from James Watt to James Black (you knew who he was all along, didn't you?). It is time to bring responsibility, accountability, power and control back home where it belongs, not just for the fish, the ferries, and the oil, but for all these things that impinge directly on Scottish culture, economics, politics, technology and society.

These arguments transcend narrow issues of productivity and economic growth, and impact on broader issues of social values. Should the provision of ferry services be seen as having social implications justifying subsidy, or should they be left for the market to provide? What should be the main driver underlying the provision of school education – high quality education for all pupils or parental choice? Should elimination of unemployment be a priority for a government, or should it simply be one of several objectives alongside control of inflation and pursuit of growth?

While economics can help look at the implications of different answers to these questions, the answers themselves ultimately depend on social and cultural values, which in turn can be contingent on time and place. Clearly there can be widely divergent answers to these questions even within countries, but for our purposes the crucial point is that the consensus view in each case can differ markedly between countries. This in turn can – and should – influence political choices.

This is uncontroversial and only becomes an issue when political choices for different countries are subsumed and constrained within a unitary state. Devolution has already begun to highlight possible fault lines where social and cultural values may differ (or at least have a differing emphasis) between Scotland and England. Should England, like Scotland, abolish bridge tolls, have free care for the elderly, and end prescription charges? There is no law, economic or otherwise, that says they should; equally there is no law that says they should not. The question is about political choices, which in turn are influenced by what the consensus in a country thinks should be priorities. Devolution has already gone some way to freeing up political choices that reflect legitimate differences in social and cultural values – or priorities – between Scotland and England. But devolution is only a half way house, what both Scotland and the rest of the UK need is the ability to take independent decisions sensitive to the particular values that the unitary state simply wallpapers over.

In the words of my *alma mater*, Fraserburgh Academy's motto, '*Sapientia Clavis Vitae*' ('Wisdom is the key of life', dummy), As for the rest, *carpe diem*. The Greeks may have had a word for it, but I confess the Romans could still turn a good phrase. And it beats 'independence by all rational and reasonable methods' hands down. QED[38]

Notes

1 McWhirter, W. (1974) *When the Black Rain Falls, Time Magazine*, April 8th. http://www.time.com/time/magazine/-article/0,9171,908536,00.html

2 ibid

3 Keynes, J. M. (1924) *A Tract on Monetary Reform*, London Macmillan, ch. 3

4 ibid

5 Keynes, J. M. (1963) Economic Possibilities for our Grand-children, in, *Essays in Persuasion*, New York: W. W. Norton & Co., pp. 358–373 (essay originally published in 1930)

6 Kay, N. M. (2002) The Barnett formula and the Squeeze, in, Calling Scotland to Account, Policy Institute, pp. 44–49

7 During a 1977 debate on Scottish and Welsh devolution, Tam Dalyell, MP for West Lothian, asked, 'For how long will English constituencies and English Honourable members tolerate... at least 119 Honourable Members from Scotland, Wales and Northern Ireland exercising an important, and probably often decisive, effect on British politics while they themselves have no say in the same matters in Scotland, Wales and Northern Ireland?' He offered his own potential situation as an example: as an MP he would be able to vote on matters affecting Blackburn, Lancashire, but not of Blackburn, West Lothian in his own constituency.

8 Commission on Scottish Devolution 2008–09, Chaired by Sir Kenneth Calman

9 Speech by Rt. Hon. Jack McConnell MSP First Minister of Scotland 10 November 2006, IPPR http://www.ippr.org.uk/uploadedFiles/events/JackMcConnell_10.11.06.pdf

10 Brown, G. and Alexander, D. A, (2008) *Stronger Together: The 21st century case for Scotland and Britain,* Fabian Ideas 621, The Fabian Society, London

11 *The Scotsman*, 13 January 2008.

12 United States Declaration of Independence, in Congress, 4 July 1776

13 Proclamation signed by the Rhodesian government, 11 November 1965

14 Devine, T. M. (2006) *The Scottish Nation, 1700–2007*, London, Penguin

15 Ibid, pp. 249–66

16 Ibid, p. 252

17 Ibid, p. 250

18 Ibid, p. 257

19 Ibid, p. 256

20 Ibid, p. 258

21 Ibid, p. 257

22 Porter, M. (1990) *The Competitive Advantage of Nations*, London, Macmillan

23 Ibid

24 See, for example, Danson, M. and G. Whittam (1998) Clustering, Innovations and Trust: the Essentials of a Clustering Strategy for Scotland, Working Paper, Department of Economics, University of Paisley; Botham, R. (1997) Inward investment and regional development; Scotland and the electronics industry. Paper to the Regional Science Association: British and Irish Section Conference, Falmouth

25 Bale K. and J. Lyons (2007) Fury As Sun Man Says Scots Sponge Off English, *Scottish Daily Record*, 13 Oct

26 Doyle, A. C. (1894) 'Silver Blaze', in *The Memoirs of Sherlock Holmes,* Gerge Newnes, London.

27 Forty-nine and half percent in Latin prelims. Fraserburgh Academy, 1963. I like to think there was a heritage and

influence of Scottish engineering precision which led to that mark being awarded

28 See, for example, *Pattern in Corporate Evolution*, Oxford University Press, 2000.

29 See especially Davie, G. E (1999) *The Democratic Intellect: Scotland and Her Universities in the 19th Century,* Edinburgh, Edinburgh University Press; Paterson, L. (2003) *Scottish Education in the 20th Century*, Edinburgh, Edinburgh University Prsss

30 If you also have difficulty finding out who he is, that underlines my point.

31 Marine and Fisheries Agency (2007) *United Kingdom Sea Fisheries Statistics 2006*, Defra Publications

32 Evidence on GERS to Scottish Parliament Finance Committee, January 2007, Neil Kay

33 See Sachs, J. D and Warner A. (2001) 'The curse of natural resources' *European Economic Review* 45 827

34 ibid

35 See: Regional Specialisation in the Long Run, Guy Michaels, October 2006 http://personal.lse.ac.uk/michaels/Michaels_Specialization_Fall_2006.pdf, Resource-Abundance and Economic Growth in the US Papyrakis, E. and Gerlagh, R. 2004 http://130.37.129.100/ivm/organisation/staff/papers/EER_resourcesUS.pdf

Does the Natural Resource Curse Apply to the United States? Cooke, C., Aadland, D. and Coupal R., May 2006 http://www.uwyo.edu/aadland/research/resourcecurse.pdf

36 *The Prince* by Nicolo Machiavelli Written c. 1505, published 1515 Translated by W. K. Marriott for the Liberty Press

37 Casson, M. (1995) *Entrepreneurship and Business Culture, Studies in the Economics of Trust Vol 1* Edward Elgar, Aldershot, p. 232

38 Quod erat demonstrandum p. 74

CHAPTER 4

Scotland and Globalisation[1]

Tom Nairn

> It often requires, perhaps, the highest effort of political wisdom, to determine when a real patriot ought to support and endeavor to re-establish the authority of the old system, and when he ought to give way to the more daring, but often dangerous spirit of innovation.
>
> Adam Smith[2]

IN APRIL 2008 the *Sunday Herald* newspaper published the latest opinion poll of the Scottish electorate, worth quoting here as a general indicator of the likely direction of events:

> Independence has taken a dramatic lead in a new opinion poll on Scotland's constitutional future. An exclusive TNS System Three poll has found that 41 per cent of Scots want the SNP government to negotiate an independence settlement, compared to 40 per cent who are opposed to breaking up the UK. The extraordinary poll results mark one of the few occasions in which independence has out-polled support for the Union.[3]

Of course such surveys fluctuate, and no-one can be sure how long such a conviction will endure. However, certain other features of the Scottish and the British Isles environment suggest strongly that this manifestation of opinion will continue, and is more likely to grow than to decrease. Adam Smith's advice quoted above is again relevant, and convincing more 'real patriots' every day. In the 18th century he was of course moving in the other direction, urging compatriots to accept and make the most of 'dangerous innovation', in the shape of Great Britain, and Union with the English. Today I'm pretty sure he would be telling them to forget about that, and go farther: globalisation is the name of the new game. And in it, Scots will again stand a better chance on their own, by standing up for themselves upon the new world stage. Let me begin by simply listing some features supporting this stance; after which I will return to the question of just when and how pro-independence views could become more stable, and even dominant – something like the 'settled will of the Scottish people' for their own state.

Evidence of Awakening

First, the poll plainly reflects recent national experience, over the years 2007 and 2008. In May 2007, the regionally devolved government of Scotland voted for an important change: the British Labour Party lost power in Scotland, for the first time since devolved government was set up in 1998, and the Scottish National Party – until quite recently an impotent sect – was able to form an administration. Though without an overall majority, as the largest single party it organised a government with support from smaller groups and independent members, under the leadership of First Minister Alex Salmond.

The fact was surprising enough but (second, and even more surprising) the administration that followed has proved both effective and popular – that is, popular in a sense that had never marked the Labour Party over its previous eight years of uninterrupted domination. One survey after another has shown this, all the more strikingly against the background of a Europe, and indeed a world, where it has become rather normal to suspect, distrust and ridicule 'politics'.

When the Holyrood Parliament was opened for business, Edwin Morgan signalled the event with a prose-poem, *Open the Doors!* What do the people want of the place?, he asked:

> A symposium of procrastinators is what they do not want...
> You are picking up a thread of pride and self-esteem
> that has been almost but not quite, oh no not quite, not ever broken or forgotten..
> When you convene you will be reconvening, with a sense of not
> wholly the power, not yet wholly the power, but a good
> sense of what was once in the honour of your grasp.[4]

However, 'something more' is now called for, not yet known but 'you will know about it when we do tell you'. In the meantime, behave with 'a good sense of what was once in the honour of your grasp'. They didn't have to wait too long. In 2007, near the 300th anniversary of surrendering statehood in 1707, the electorate provided a counter-case to the anti-politics of the time, by voting for an untried political vehicle, and a year later being reasonably happy with the results. In spite of all the standard denunciations of Nationalism (bypassed, doom-laden, parochial, racialist and so on) a National Party has not only won regional power but embarked on a program of moderate but consistent reform – a social-democratic drive towards persuading its electors that more complete self-government is both needed for its programme of change to continue, and attainable.

The most reliable analysis of this unprecedented situation has probably come from Iain Macwhirter, the *Sunday Herald*'s (and Scotland's) most serious political journalist. Writing one year after the Nationalists came into office, he said:

> It took a Nationalist government to discover the power of devolution... The SNP have set a blistering if sometimes chaotic pace. I recall arriving at Bute House (official residence of the First Minister) for a meeting with Salmond... and finding him in the state room surrounded

> by young aides, piles of paper and empty coffee cups. Civil servants scurried in and out, as if they were living in the early days of a better country. It was never like this under the previous management.

A quiet earthquake had happened, and was continuing – even escalating – a year later. It had started from the voters, and altered even the civil servants. Macwhirter goes on to describe the country left behind. 'Great Britain' has turned out to be the least of the new and better country's problems:

> There could be troubles ahead. But the one thing that hasn't caused significant trouble so far has been relations with Westminster. Yes there have been spats... but no real bust ups. Many people expected that the SNP in office would spend much more of its time picking fights with UK ministries, blaming London for Scotland's ills and turning the Scottish Executive into a £30 billion battering ram for independence. It hasn't happened.

On the contrary, the Nationalists have been able to convert a wider disillusionment into a quite unexpectedly positive endorsement for a necessarily vague 'new deal' on the smaller stage of Scotland.

> In the past, independence was a vague and distant possibility; a world of fantasy politics. Now, with a dynamic nationalist administration in office, it is possible to see what independence might actually look like in practice. Across Scotland surprising people, like the Scottish billionaire Tom Hunter, and Stephen Purcell, the Labour leader of Glasgow City Council, are talking seriously about a referendum on independence.

Sunday Herald readers are of course hardly representative of general opinion. But it may be of significance that in the opinion poll accompanying Macwhirter's article, no fewer than *90 per cent* of respondents saw the referendum as a good idea.

United Kingdom: for 'decline' read 'defeat'

The third, most important background feature of today's dilemma emerges from between the lines of all these arguments. 'Westminster' (the United Kingdom state) has made a poor showing over the past two years, for deeper historical and structural reasons than policy disputes can convey. At the same time as actual blood has been shed in Iraq and Afghanistan, by Labour Government support for a consistently unpopular war, something analogous has unfolded on the metaphorical and collective emotional plane. The life-blood has been rapidly draining out of United Kingdom identity, and led to a chronic anaemia that most citizen/subjects now feel in their bones. Prime Minister Brown is an example of the sort of fiercely pro-British Scot who once predominated, and whose attitudes were simply taken for granted. Such attitudes didn't vanish overnight with de-colonisation; but over a generation they have vanished none the less, in a terminal thousand-cuts process, little affected by London bluster and pretension (if not encouraged by it). The last episode of the latter has been Brown's own painful and perfectly futile campaign to revive 'Britishness' over the years 2005 to 2008.

It must also be kept in mind that such collapse has touched all parts of the United Kingdom. Scottish separation may become its most dramatic result. However, different forms of the same palsy have affected Wales, Northern Ireland *and England itself*. In Wales, a Nationalist-Labour Party coalition has assumed power in the Welsh Assembly, aiming at enhanced self-government by 2011 (also via a referendum). In Northern Ireland, the traditionally passionate adhesion of the Protestant community to Crown-land Britain has weakened to the extent of allowing an even more surprising regional alliance of forces – between the Protestants of Democratic Unionism and Sinn Féin, the pro-Republican Catholic movement led by Gerry Adams and Martin McGuiness. This notably hybrid regime is supported by both London and Dublin states, the former weakened by disintegration, the latter empowered by economic success.

Thus Scottish moves towards statehood are taking place in an environment that has itself changed beyond recognition since the times of Margaret Thatcher and the younger Tony Blair. Just as in the 1980s the old Soviet East-European imperium 'imploded' rather than merely suffering defeat from outside, so in the 2010s and 2020s, the 17th century British Kingdom looks like collapsing into its component parts through internal inertia, identity-foundering and the need to build alternative political vehicles. Consistent failure to reform the central state and constitution has compelled the components of this multi-national order to reform themselves. Over a whole generation, the after-shocks of an Empire in retreat had remarkably little impact – less than the comparable process in France. But this was a mixed blessing, because it enabled the core of the British *ancien régime* state to survive. Yet death is no less certain for having been prolonged by genteel 'decline' – and also, by increasingly absurd efforts at redemption.[5]

Such efforts have of course relied upon the UK's 'special relationship' with American power, as if the latter's expansion could somehow save (or even reverse) the final loss of British world-power and status. One should not underestimate the strength of this delusion. For one thing, it helps explain 'devolution'. At the end of last century, both Labourites and Liberal-Democrats remained so convinced of traditional multi-national stability and continuity that the risk of allowing some 'Home Rule' to peripheral nations could be taken – accompanied by resonant assurances this would *strengthen* all-British identity and institutions.

What such trumpet-blasts hid was actually the staged *defeat* of Britannia during the Cold War decades, and her transformation into a parody of previous glory, through self-colonization and subservience. The ideology of 'decline' also helped to misrepresent this fall. 'Decline' can be read as suggesting, even implying, the possibility of revival and reanimation, via minor victories like the South Atlantic War to recapture the Falkland Islands, or even through forms of culture like popular music and the arts. Outright military and political defeat like that suffered by France in 1940, or later in Algeria, or by the Axis states in 1945–46, is something quite different. There, reform and new starts were determined by circumstances, not by ideological programmes and 'think-tanks'. By contrast, it is the latter that have signalled British-imperial attempts to remain 'great' from the 1950s onwards: one 'vision' after another, culminating in Blair's 'New Labourism' at the end of the century.[6]

In the Wider World

Fourth, and perhaps most important, is the background of 'globalisation'. UK decrepitude may be the most obvious causative factor in the break-up trend; but one should never forget how it has intersected with universal trends like Neo-liberal capitalist expansion, in which British governments have played such a prominent part. Tony Blair followed Margaret Thatcher as an apostle of globalisation in just that sense. The 'decline' discussed earlier has been compensated for by loud ideological assertiveness, in Europe as well as under the special relationship with two American Presidencies. London has over the relevant period been more than a camp-follower: Shakespearian Herald and persuasive Royal Messenger would seem more appropriate, relaying the messages that Charles de Gaulle originally identified as 'Anglo-Saxon'. Right-wing Anglo-Saxon historical materialism might be the more complete title: that is, the victorious counterpart of a pseudo-materialism still deployed by many socialist and communist parties and governments up to 1989 (and still enjoying life-after-death under the Chinese state). Antonio Gramsci called the Leninist version *egemonia,* and urged the Left to conquer souls through it, as a desirable prelude to power and government. However, capitalist apostles produced their own version of the lesson, and practised *egemonia* rather effectively over the 1980s and 1990s – even if, in the end, they have illustrated certain limitations of the formula as well.

I mentioned above how identity-haemorrhage has affected heartland-English opinion. The most striking expression of this has been a series of surveys over 2006–07 showing majorities of English opinion *indifferent* to the possibility of Scottish separation. In earlier times, most passionate intensity had appeared on the 'Unionist' side, displaying an indignant consciousness of the sacred character of 18th century all-British institutions and attitudes. Clearly, that sacral nature was the 'life-blood' that has now all but drained away. It was not at all the same thing as what has taken its place: *reasonable* arguments over the advantages of preserving links, or the 'good side' of co-existence in a single framework – more or less the same as in most debates about European Union. Few nationalists in Scotland, Wales or Ireland would dissent from such positions.

They are simply arguing for a new, better foundation for developing these 'good sides' to amity and cooperation. Within an antique 'common framework' visibly – indeed determinedly – incapable of serious constitutional modernisation, *societal* modernisation was none the less carried forward. Society has been forced to 'fall back' on resources still present and potentially active, though side-lined for all too long. And it has done so all the more easily, because many features of globalisation appear to *favour* such changes, most evidently among *smaller* political units, regions and populations 'left behind' by the forced march of 19th and 20th century state-formation.[7]

To grasp the oddity of the UK and Scottish situations more thoroughly, perhaps more theory is required. The most interesting recent one has been presented by Professor Fred Halliday of the London School of Economics, in the OpenDemocracy website of 13 May 2008 (www.opendemocracy.net): 'The Politics of Failure'. Today's globe confronts any observer with a range of events disturbingly like old-fashioned empire or colonialism: from Hawaii to Wales, as it were, via West Papua, Taiwan, Tibet, Kashmir, Kurdistan, Iraq, Darur, the Basque lands, Québec and many others. And yet, most of the dominant states involved deny being old-fashioned in that sense – that is, unlike (e.g.) France in the Maghreb, Britain in India, or Japan in China or Korea. Halliday argues they are (or perceive themselves as) in effect 'tidying up' the globalising world.

The bigger states are still maintaining their right to have *not less* than the entitlements handed down from the previous age of nationalism and empire. The court of global opinion and the magistrates of the United Nations no longer recognise nation-*grabbing*; but nation-*retaining* and (of course) improving may be different. Those who failed their chances of independence in the main round (up to the 1960s) may today find themselves threatened by impoundment or restraint orders, via assertions of such legitimate priority and right. Such legitimacy may itself be dubious, grey, feigned or even absurd – still, as Halliday warns, the 'what-we-have-we-hold' bunch is for the moment likely to prevail. Hence his counsel of 'realistic pessimism' over these issues: short of breakdown and crazed excesses (as in Indonesian East Timor) they're likely to hold on to recognition.

Halliday uses mainly the case of Tibet and China for illustration. But examples like the Kurds and Turkey, the East-Timorese or West-Papuans against Indonesia, or the Kashmiris against both India and Pakistan would be equally useful. So (I would argue) is the case of peripheral-nation Britain versus the United Kingdom. What counts is, as he puts it, 'respect for regional and cultural rights within a democratic framework'. So far the latter has been either absent, feeble or dubious in most having-and-holding polities, with important exceptions like India and Canada. The case of the USA lies in the 'dubious' category: in the year 2000 it failed to elect a President, and a failing state had to be rescued by High Court manipulation. And the UK? In 2005 the British unreformed constitution imposed a parliamentary majority founded on 21½ per cent of the vote. Any realistic pessimism will of course foresee the same or worse occurring in 2010, and thereafter. This is surely at least equally 'dubious': an anti-democratic *norm* staunchly upheld – having-and-holding by custom and sacred antecedents.

Loose ends, breakaways, democratic awakenings and new starts depend upon a break with such habits – in effect upon 'rights within a democratic framework' being better served by (e.g.) an independent Tibet than as part of an autocratic, Party-ruled China. There may indeed be cases where populations come to accept that 'major goals of democracy, respect and economic prosperity' are best served by remaining part of the larger entity (Halliday mentions Catalonia, Bavaria, Crete and California). But that in turn depends upon larger entities doing far more than just being there, and sticking to their habitual fixations. It will depend, surely, on their *reforming themselves* to justify retention, or any re-imposition of rights and responsibilities. In times of democratic warming, resigned nods and acquiescent grunts from the UN and 'international opinion' will no longer suffice. For the failing UK, anaemic indifference of the majority won't be enough; it may be better than repression, but is nothing like the positive drive needed for effective retention (let alone rejuvenation). On *this* display-board, the democratic credentials being offered by the head-strong peripheries (including Halliday's own Ireland) are surely more impressive.

Democratic Republicanism

One big advantage of Halliday's speculation is that it compels one to think more concretely about alternatives – outside the existing '-isms'. It's no longer enough to aspire vaguely towards 'democratic nationalism', whether among the tidying-up majorities, or the aspiring subordinates. Any 'framework' worth the name will consist of institutions; and the institution that counts here is surely the democratic *republic.*[8]

In the wake of short-cut Socialism's failure, 'Republicanism' can no longer be taken for granted. It has to find new significance, as the 'public factor' now facing the foreseeable common future of capitalism-management. However, neither the former nor the latter are the same everywhere; globalising unity both renders existing contrasts more striking *and* calls for further differentiation, to counter-balance the elements of homogeneity that have inevitably been made centre-stage. Imperialist conflict and the Cold War posited generally divergent answers to human 'species-being', and imagined the coat of many colours at last dissolving into one or other wardrobe-'world'. This choice has disappeared, but the colours have not.

Scotland is just one place where they are re-appearing: an early-modern version of take-over agreed by the old Scottish ruling class in 1707 is being challenged, and may very soon be decisively reversed. Halliday suspects this may not come about, but gives no reasons why. It remains difficult to imagine, let alone predict, any transmutation of central power in the United Kingdom. In the circumstances outlined above, surely a shift of the centre would be needed, more thorough and ambitious than devolution and (obviously) supported by the overwhelming English majority. But there is *no sign whatever* of such a new 'democratic framework' emerging.

There are of course groups and campaigns in favour of an English Parliament, invariably accompanied by demands for an equivalent Little-England democracy. And the Liberal Democrats have urged proportional representation for decades. But some recent indicators suggest these have been stalled, and may even be in retreat. A counter-revolution took place in a recent by-election in the constituency of Crewe & Nantwich, where thousands of disabused Labourites must have passed from one 'main party' to the other – in effect, a reinforcement of the *ancien régime*. At any foreseeable general election this would leave David Cameron's New Conservatives in charge of whatever piecemeal changes are made to assuage English opinion – undoubtedly in the interest of restoration and the sacred Anglo-British identity and structures.

At the same time, it's quite possible that most citizens of Wales, Scotland and Northern Ireland would indeed support (for example) a *confederal* rearrangement of the United Kingdom, a new 'republicanism' based on some fairer representative system. The latter might even leave the multi-national monarchy in a constitutionally-defined symbolic place – as in

Scandinavia. However, that would need prolonged preparation and bi-partisan support, as well as a referendum – the kind of all-round new start in which Anglo-British public opinion remains quite uninterested. As long as that remains true, break-up will be the realist option; in Albert O. Hirschmann's classical terminology, Exit will have it over Loyalty.[9] Naturally the former will be opposed by paid-up members of the Have-and-Hold Club, like America, Spain, Indonesia, Turkey and other states.

However, the has-been anguish may not endure for ever. These days, women find their way into the crustiest and most inveterate of clubs. On the global stage, the equivalent of feminism is what one might call the stowaways' club: that is, the transformative movement of the small and small-to-medium polities who never had empires, found themselves marginalised or 'absorbed', and now find themselves expected to carry on serving a globalisation led by Great or would-be Great 'powers' having-and-holding on to their earlier gains. It was taken for granted *they* would be on the bridge, and not down in steerage-class or the porthole-less cabins and bunk-rooms for recipient nationalities. I argued recently that, with its constant change and shake-up, globalisation may be far more favourable to the latter than previously imagined.[10] They are ceasing to be 'meek', and looking for alliances capable of giving 'voice' and guaranteeing presence in circumstances where so much (though not yet enough) that was solid is melting into air.

Unpredicted Voices

One constant, nagging argument that has rumbled on over generations is the 'lack of self-confidence' of the Scots, an apparently chronic reluctance or inability to take initiatives, or claim leadership. In recent years Carol Craig's *The Scots' Crisis of Confidence* (2005) has summed up this debate, and claimed that the 'crisis' has been one of civil society, of emotions and attitudes distinct from (and deeper than) questions of politics and constitutionality. Hence it calls for psychological or communal therapy, rather than statehood or shifts of allegiance.

The author attributed Scottish diffidence and lieutenant-mentality to the effects of religious reformation, rather than to the surrender of statehood and the prolonged 'self-colonisation' of the imperial centuries.

Since the 2007 election and its results, I think such conclusions can reasonably be doubted. It now looks much more likely that restoration of fuller self-government, although not in itself a cure, may be an absolutely necessary condition of redressing the overall balance that serious therapy requires. 'Not quite, oh no not quite, not ever broken or forgotten...' was the way Edwin Morgan put it in the Holyrood verses I quoted earlier; but we can now see and feel how deeply the *restoration* of that grasp, and its associated 'honour' touches and affects the great majority, and upon all levels of their being. 'Restoration' of independence isn't a return to the past, but a psychological and emotional use of that past to generate 'self-confidence' in the present, for the sake of the future.

On a more personal note, it may be worth observing that I have not emerged unaffected from so many recent political and constitutional shifts. Often in academic circles where theories of nationalism get discussed, and new versions of cosmopolitanism are in vogue, I have heard it said that '-isms' like these matter little to non-intellectuals, and don't affect deeper emotions and attitudes. As someone forced into distance from my own background since the year 2000, and enjoying only periodical or spasmodic re-immersion, I can only say I have not found this to be the case. The formative culture has grown more, not less important under such conditions; and the 2007 events have had an impact much greater than I would previously have imagined. 'Imagined Communities' is Ben Anderson's famous name for the countries that forge us, going on to live in our nervous systems as well as our polite conversations and theories. And another great Scottish poet has put it all much better than I could, in a few lines I remember being deeply moved by many years ago, without grasping just why. I perceive now it was because he ended with one of the greatest lines in contemporary Scottish verse. Iain Crichton Smith's '*Two Girls Singing*' described them singing their hearts out on a Glasgow bus last century, 'through late November running, by yellow lights tormented, darkness falling'. But the sense of the songs wasn't the point in this 'strange awakening', for no reason but themselves, 'for miles and miles together':

> ... and it wasn't the words or tune. It was the singing.
> It was the human sweetness in that yellow,
> the unpredicted voices of our kind.[11]

Notes

1 The title of a talk originally given in France, at the University of Burgundy in Dijon. My thanks are due to Professors Agnès Alexandre-Collier and Keith Dixon for the invitation back to a town and region greatly loved at an earlier time in my life.

2 ADAM SMITH, *The Theory of Moral Sentiments* (1959), pp. 230–3 of 1976 Profile edition, Edited by Raphael & Macfie

3 13 April 2008.

4 See the Scottish Parliament website: http://www.scottish.parliament.uk/vli/holyrood/projHistory/EdwinMorgan.htm – 2008–02–10

5 On this general theme an outstanding recent overview of state-formation can also be quoted in evidence: Philip Roeder's *Where Nation-States Come From: Institutional Change in an Age of Nationalism* (Princeton, 2007). The author's argument is that East-bloc implosion was guided more by the prior existence of state-like or national *institutions* than by ethnicity, tongue or religious beliefs. Scotland is of course a further example of the thesis: the 'civic-historical' has weighed much more heavily than an often over-estimated ethnic and folkloric past.

6 For an overview of the process, see *The British Regulatory State: High Modernism and Hyper-innovation*, by Michael Moran (Oxford, 2007). 'Devolution' was in this author's sense an episode of despairing 'hyper-innovation', whose final result has been a heightening of *ancien régime* autocracy, Britain's part in a general Neo-liberal turn towards authoritarianism – as e.g. in Bush's Neo-Conservatism or John Howard's Liberal Coalition regime in Australia, from 1996 to 2007.

7 I put forward this aspect of the changes at greater length in an earlier 'Edinburgh Lecture' delivered on 4 March 2008, at the invitation of Scotland's First Minister. See *Scottish Left Review, Issue No. 46, 'Globalization's New Deal'*. www.scottish leftreview.org/uk

8 A valuable overview of recent thinking on republicanism is provided by Serge Audier's *Les théories de la république* (La Découverte, Paris, 2004), and a relevant history can be found in Jean-Fabien Spitz's *Le moment républicain en France* (Gallimard, Paris, 2005).

9 *Exit, Voice and Loyalty: Responses to Decline* (1970 and 2007) BY WHOM AND WHERE?

10 See the 'Edinburgh Lecture' of 4 March 2008, a version of which has appeared on OpenDemocracy for 7-03.2008: www.opendemocracy.net.' Globalization and Nationalism: the New Deal'

11 *Collected Poems*, Manchester, 2000, p. 48

CHAPTER 5

An English Voice in Scotland

Betty Davies

This is the testimony of a prominent English business-woman who has lived and worked in Scotland for over 40 years. Her long relationship with the leading Nationalist Douglas Henderson, led Betty Davies, finally, at the end of his life, to support the cause of Scottish independence.

In this moving and challenging memoir, she explains why.

I CAME TO WORK in Scotland from the Guildhall School of Music and Drama, inspired by the Edinburgh Festival, excited by the opportunities the country presented – and because the '60s were the time to make things happen.

I stepped off the overnight sleeper on an icy cold February morning, dragging a weighty suitcase to a waiting taxi and emerged from Waverley Station to be stunned by the sight of one of the most dramatic skylines in Europe. The architects of Edinburgh had created a stage set on which to play out its history. In those brief moments I was not to know then that 40 years later a historic new drama would be enacted, and that I would have a seat in the stalls.

With nothing in my pocket but a job offer and a good friend who arranged for me to stay with a family whose daughter was away mountaineering and whose room, at the top of a winding staircase at Sir Walter Scott's house in George Square, could be mine for a few weeks until I found my feet, I opened my suitcase and took stock.

Within a few months, as PRO (Press Relations Officer) of the Scottish Gas Board, I was organising an opera at the Edinburgh

Festival, now documented as the first event to be sponsored by corporate industry.

Next came the shop, Campus in the Grassmarket – 'Clever clothes for clever girls' – enticing customers looking for minis and ball gowns, as well as the down-and-outs waiting for the hostels to open! Campus spread its wings to other university cities. There followed design, concert organisation, the Traverse Theatre, STV, Harris Tweed, the Edinburgh Theatre Workshop, much corporate design and management, and much more. It all sounds rather rosy, but it was not always what it seemed.

Life in Scotland was not easy for me. In those early days I bore the painful barbs of many xenophobic work colleagues: 'Here two days and already you're empire building'; 'Your work is beautiful, but your voice is too English' – the response of the BBC's icon of Scottish radio, George Bruce, who auditioned me.

Thirty years later, I invited him to address an entranced audience at the RSA about his first meeting with the poet Norman Soutar. When I reminded him of his words, he said: 'It wouldn't happen now.' But it does!

I soon learned that although my family name was Stevenson and my background was strictly Presbyterian, resonating with the values highly regarded in Scotland, my RP (Received Pronunciation) English meant that if I were to be accepted, it would be as a well-intentioned guest in a country that I soon came to love as my own.

A hectic work schedule allowed little time for political distractions. As I travelled round Scotland in those first few months I was shocked by the unemployment in Glasgow and by the abject poverty in the housing schemes of the central belt. Coming from a thriving industrial city in the Midlands of England, I wondered: Why was Scotland so attached to Labour? I didn't understand it then and I fail to understand it now.

Why were the disaffected, the bitter and disillusioned blaming the English when they should be aiming their verbal fire power at the negligence of their own MPs? Surely there had to be a change?

Change came slowly and then gathered momentum. In

November 1967, on the very night we opened the Glasgow Campus shop, Winifred Ewing, the charismatic Glasgow lawyer, won the Hamilton by-election. The change was beginning.

Some years later, having supported the patriotism and political acumen of my long term companion and business partner, the late Douglas Henderson MP, and having listened to his daily reports on the political arguments waging in Westminster and later Holyrood, I could hardly escape the conclusion that the present constitutional arrangements had to change.

Douglas was one of the seven SNP MPs first elected to Westminster in 1974, their Chief Whip, and a man highly regarded for his negotiating skills and burning zeal for Independence. He deprecated a Devolved Parliament as a distraction that might just in the long term present a viable alternative – and therefore be politically unwise. I conclude that his political thinking then has resonance now.

Douglas's untimely death in 2006 robbed Scotland of one of its most astute and prescient politicians and the SNP's most formidable orator. His death robbed me of a loving, generous-hearted and witty companion who completely understood that I loved my country every bit as much as he loved his. Political discussion was often rather colourful but on one question there was always total agreement (we defended each other's beliefs) and that was on the love and pride of country, heritage and culture. We wanted to strive to better our countries. And all the time I was learning so much about Scotland. It was an enriching experience.

During almost 30 years of an action-packed political and business relationship Douglas never once asked me where I cast my vote. It was an uncrossed boundary.

Even at the very end of his life Douglas was harrowed by his sense of failure to live long enough to see Independence realised. It was then, in the last few hours together that I promised him that in the forthcoming election for the Scottish Parliament I would vote SNP – and that his lifetime endeavour would have my continuing support.

Why was I able to make this decision? Because the ebb and flow of the changing interests of England and Scotland had dominated my political thinking for a past decade. I had watched with dismay the political ennui that engulfed and almost anaesthetised voters in England. So many things that in the past were regarded highly, the pillars on which love and pride in country were structured, became under threat and in danger of crumbling.

Education in mainstream England was in free fall. Excelling in scholarship is in danger of losing out to the new currency of mediocrity and political correctness. The teaching of history – that so inspires confidence and underpins the understanding of our legal, social and cultural systems – has fleeting exposure in the curriculum. Music, poetry and the humanising subjects often became available only to those whose families could afford to pay for them.

For the less academic, there is now little time or opportunity for participation in physical education and games. Sluggishness and juvenile obesity is a diet problem which, like so many things, once the prerogative and responsibility of parents, must be managed by the state. The inheritors of years of poor education and no job prospects are a third generation disenfranchised by a corroding lack of social and communication skills. This is a heart-breaking situation, which desperately needs to be addressed.

Throughout history England has been accepting and absorbing immigrants from many countries. As Labour drastically cut the Custom controls at many ports of entry in Britain early in its term of office, unchecked and unmanaged immigration now causes further strain in England's overcrowded cities as demands on overburdened hospitals, schools and housing services increase. In areas of high unemployment the ugly spectre of racial tension rears. The Government's statistics on demographic change appear to be guesswork – or are unavailable.

The Labour Government at Westminster, against all advice by both magistrates and police has extended the drinking hours, causing the spewing forth of thousands upon thousands of young drunks on to the streets long after midnight. Gambling (to fill Gordon Brown's tax coffers) has become more acceptable, almost encouraged, and in England and also Scotland drug and knife crime daily threaten the lives of so many innocent young people. The men and women who police our streets are heroes charged with an almost impossible task, and there are far too few of them.

This Labour Government has been the progenitor of the cynical philosophy: If it works, change it; to change it, throw money at it. Ill conceived legislation hurriedly brought in as a response to bad headlines has often been abandoned as unworkable within a matter of a few months. Many millions have been spent on consultants installing billion pound computers with open-ended contracts that leave the taxpayer footing the bills when the systems crash, or never even start.

Ministers of the Crown now stand accused of negligent practices that cannot ensure the safety of private information on thousands of its citizens, and yet initiate draconian laws that impose restrictions on the freedom of law abiding citizens. The road to hell is indeed paved with good intentions.

The legacy of this Labour Government is a deeply disillusioned electorate who now, in a time of economic uncertainty, no longer trusts what politicians tell them. This is a very serious indictment on a government. In England there is increasing bitterness that unwelcome parliamentary decisions have been shored up by MPs from Scottish constituencies who, with the exception of the SNP MPs, vote on matters of English legislation which are devolved to Scotland. This runs counter to common justice.

The Prime Minister's ill conceived campaign to enforce a greater sense of Britishness – 'I'm Scottish and proud to be British' – received short shrift in many parts of England, where they are as equally proud to be English as the Scots to be Scots. It is no doubt well intended, but is a concept that suggests that the UK is like a giant 'pop' concert that can be made to play the same tune. Clearly it does not.

Now faced with a calamitous downturn in the polls and escalating problems in the economy, Ministers, who though they preach good social conscience, fail to convince that they are able to make it work in practice. Over the years there has been a sinister rise of the professional politician, someone who has learned the jargon of persuasion but has never collected a wage packet, estimated a job, read a contract or managed a business.

Gordon Brown, the new Chancellor of the Exchequer in 1997, inherited a reasonable economic situation from his Conservative predecessor Kenneth Clarke. But Brown sold off half the Treasury's gold reserves at a low price[1] to fund a spending spree for needy public services, without creating an infrastructure to ensure competent implementation. Now that our economy is under serious threat by further turbulence and instability in the financial sector – the coffers are bare. Has anyone seen Prudence? Prudence was obviously greatly overrated.

This Labour administration, with all its good intentions and high mindedness came into power intending to transform Britain – only to spin out of control because of its inability to manage the edifices it created. The tragedy is that Gordon Brown is unable to see what he has done; does he even want to look? His absence from the recent Glasgow East by-election said it all.

The recent broken promise to allow a referendum on the Treaty of the European Union was a serious breach of faith. His behaviour in arriving to sign the Treaty, after the departure of the other European leaders, suggested embarrassment rather than conviction. These actions do not go unnoticed.

Why is this Labour Government in such default? Some of the rot set in, of course, during the last years of the previous Conservative government, but the major demise has been perpetuated and accelerated by a New Labour administration which seems to have lost sight of its ethical principles and the basic moralities of the old Labour movement.

What is apparent is that the paralysis of the current Westminster Government has brought about a shared dissatisfaction among both the English and the Scots, thus creating a shared dilemma. For all his grand and often repeated rhetoric, Gordon Brown has managed to alienate both the English and his own countrymen.

Here in Scotland many people who had never voted SNP before watched with dismay as their devolved Government led by Labour, with Lib Dem assistance, fumbled its way through eight years of being Westminster's carpetbaggers. The administration was in tatters.

The Opposition of SNP MSPs led by Alex Salmond, Nicola Sturgeon and John Swinney clearly stood head and shoulders above their Labour counterparts. If Labour in Scotland was to be deposed, we had at last been offered a workable alternative.

As I and many, many thousands of others put our crosses for the first time in the box that produced the majority of one for the SNP, the significance of that vote will never ever be forgotten.

Scotland had at last rejected the dead hand of Labour and now had an articulate, clever and industrious group of men and women who the voters hope will work hard for the good of their country.

I shall never forget when I heard the result. Moira Salmond hailed me from a taxi as I was walking up The Mound. 'Betty, we've won! Alex has just left by helicopter to see the Queen – wouldn't Douglas be pleased?'

Then the tears came.

Scotland has led the way in ridding itself of a moribund Labour administration. Over the border as the former 'Iron Chancellor' sadly metamorphoses into a crumbling Prime Minister, have the electorate in England finally decided that they too have had enough?

There is now little confidence in the Westminster Parliament's ability to manage the affairs of state and the government departments. In England a bewildered electorate at first inspired, then betrayed by Tony Blair was minded to give

Gordon Brown a fair chance to remedy a seriously damaged situation. But these millions of electors are now deeply uncertain and many of my countrymen fear for the future. The English electorate is now truly 'Browned off'.

Gordon Brown is a dedicated politician, and a man of gravitas who seems to perform well on a world stage. When playing at home, however, he acts like a leading actor who is either in the wrong play, or has forgotten his lines. For all our sakes and for his, the curtain should now fall on what is a major tragedy for a sincere man.

The question now must be: Can the SNP govern convincingly? They have made an excellent start and the sceptics are beginning to warm to this Government. The performance of Alex Salmond and his ministers, particularly Nicola Sturgeon as Health Minister, has been most impressive. For a Scottish Minister of Health to receive not one but two standing ovations from GPs from England for her stance at the BMA's Annual Conference in defending the publicly funded National Health Service says a great deal about their views on her Westminster counterparts.

The electorate in Scotland is watching and listening to its SNP-led Devolved Administration with hope and enthusiasm.

The people of Scotland see that the SNP's success, led by Alex Salmond an outstanding First Minister with a refreshing 'hands on approach' is heralding a new mix of political thought and representation, from which should emerge a credible mission to shape Scotland's future for its own people. At last, and only with a tiny majority, this is being achieved.

Will my colleagues who supported other parties in the past and the SNP in 2007, do so again? They may. Although they may or may not vote for Independence in a Referendum, they seem sufficiently pleased with the early performance of their Government. But one thing is certain – this historic win for the SNP in Scotland has focussed the minds of the Labour Party in England 'to think again'. And it has provided a clear way ahead for Scotland.

As Gordon Brown dithers with his chronic uncertainty,

David Cameron has the opportunity to establish a credible alternative to Labour in England. Unacceptable as it may be to his voters in Scotland – now represented by only one Tory Member in Westminster – he must also address the continuing anomaly of MPs representing Scottish constituencies but able to vote on issues which are devolved to the Scottish Parliament. As he now examines with his MPs the new measures being proposed I wish them well in their deliberation, but the underlying issue of England's relationship with Scotland needs confronting.

He needs to consider! If at the next General Election the SNP secures between 20 and 25 seats in a Parliament that does not win a decisive majority, then the SNP will be able to dictate the political agenda for a United Kingdom government, powerless to move without SNP support. This is not an impossible scenario.

During my life in Scotland I have watched the Scots rediscovering and enthusiastically engaging in their own culture, whilst in England the wealth and diversity of her artistic heritage is neglected and in danger of being lost. Freed from the largely Labour and Independent political representation of Wales and Scotland at Westminster, separatism might allow the English to re-connect with her distinct and rich cultural heritage in music, poetry and literature before it is lost forever. England should raise her hopes and her standards. Without sounding too much like Dr Johnson, this could be a joyful prospect.

The cataclysmic rejection of Labour votes in Glasgow East has driven home to an astonished country that it is Scotland that is writing the agenda for change. Following that vote Simon Jenkins wrote in *The Sunday Times*: 'An autonomous Scotland, a country as big as Denmark, should liberate the English parliament to enjoy politics freed of the alien encumbrance of Scottish seats. It should liberate English politics, and especially the Labour party, from the distortion of 50 Scottish socialists, indelibly linked to old fashioned politics of public spending.' These are sentiments I share.

My dear Douglas was right. The Labour administration

under Prime Minister Callaghan, that Douglas's vote deposed in 1979, believed that by embracing devolution Scotland would have a sleeping tiger that Labour could tame. Labour now realises, 30 years on, that the tiger has awoken, and it has woken to a new and brighter dawn. And this is some tiger! Some dawn!

Scotland is a remarkable country with its own distinctive artistic and cultural identity and heritage. Those who come to live here do so because they seek a better quality of life. They should support this country's heritage and its future.

Three hundred years of the Act of Union is but a small step in the long, long history of these islands. The Act heralded, in spite of very real differences, a change for the good, establishing the United Kingdom as a force of enlightenment and good governance in the world. It did so under a monarchy, a constitutional beacon that is still the envy of many. This is a cause for celebration.

Yet – we now live in a state that in the last 40 years has demographically altered beyond recognition. To treasure and develop our differing cultures and to meet challenging economic demands, not least from the emerging economies of Brazil, China and India, will inevitably require dramatic change.

We must move forward with courage, with confidence, and with goodwill. Above all we must accept the right of all the people in these islands to seek both good governance and self determination.

Notes

1 cf. cf. Watt H. and Winnett R., 'Goldfinger Brown's £2 billion blunder in the bullion market' (2007), *The Sunday Times*, 15 April

Postscript

Replies to people who have doubts about Scottish independence.

1 **Would the disentanglement of Scotland from the UK be a long and expensive process?**

After Devolution we are already about half-way there. Even under the Union we retained many of our important institutions such as our legal system and important aspects of Scottish administration have been managed for years by the Scottish Office. Even without such advantages many long submerged European nations have recently become successful independent states without difficulty. There is no reason to suppose that there would be any particular problem in our own case

2 **The problems which mainly concern many people in Scotland are such matters as crime, street violence, addiction to drugs or alcohol, lack of jobs, rising costs, poor housing. Would independence help to solve them?**

There are of course no magic cures, but small states do have an advantage in dealing with such problems. Their parliaments and governments are close to the people and can take decisions and act quickly. In the British state we are only about a 10th of the population and most attention, naturally and democratically, is given to the interests of the majority. Our problems may differ from theirs in nature or degree.

3 **An independent Scotland would need is own army, navy, air force and diplomatic service. Can we afford them?**

We do not get such services at present without cost because part of the taxes which we pay in Scotland helps to finance them. They are therefore partly Scottish owned and we shall be entitled to a share on independence. Scotland would not then aspire, like Britain, to the role of a nuclear-armed great power. Our own requirements would be much more modest and reasonable, similar to those of our small European neighbours such as Denmark. The cost might even be less than we at present contribute to the British establishment

4 **Is Scotland too poor and too small to prosper with independence?**

Not in the least. As demonstrated in Independence is the Answer, the small independent countries in Europe are among the most prosperous in the world. Recent research by the National Science Foundation of the United States reached the conclusion that Denmark, which is smaller than Scotland in size and population, is the happiest of all countries. Our oil alone would make an independent Scotland very wealthy. It will not last for ever, but long enough to establish a capital fund as a guarantee of future prosperity. Scotland is rich too in other resources, fish, minerals, agriculture, and wind and tidal power. It has an educated and skilful population with a rich tradition in industry and scientific discovery

5 **Is Scotland too small and too weak to survive in a potentially hostile world?**

It is not the small countries, but the larger ones with great power ambitions which are particularly vulnerable to military involvement. The British involvement in the disastrous Iraq war is an example. An independent Scotland, along with the other small countries of Europe, would not be a threat to others nor a provocation to terrorist attack.

6 **Would an independent Scotland be isolated in the world?**

On the contrary, independence would enable us to establish, or recover, our own direct relations with the rest of the world and enable us to become a member of international organisations such as the European Union and the United Nations.

7 **Would independence mean the end of our long association and friendship with England?**

Certainly not. We should both remain members of the European Union with free movement and free trade. There would be no barriers to the continuation of cross-border movements, friendships, and relationships of all kinds. In addition many of the tensions involved in the present devolution arrangements would be removed. This includes such problems as Scottish members of the Westminster Parliament being free to vote on policies which affect only England; and English suspicions (even if mistaken) that some of their taxes are used to subsidise Scotland. An independent Scotland as a member of international organisations such as the EU would be able to express and defend our own interests and points of view, but on many questions Scotland and England would be able to support one another. Our relations with England would be strengthened, not weakened, by the removal of the problems which disturb our present relationship.

8 **The SNP would have a political monopoly in an independent Scotland, which would ultimately lead to a one-party state. We'd lose all parliamentary debate and deliberation.**

It could be said that in an independent Scotland Labour could equally have a political monopoly, as the last devolved administration did for two terms. The monopoly by one party is extremely unlikely in an independent Scotland and members of an independent Scotland will not be in thrall to an English parliament in a way that that last Labour-led administration was.

The long crusade of the SNP is to achieve independence, not a super one party state of SNP representatives. What the SNP has been able to do is to convince the electorate that the one party state of Labour in Scotland for eight years has had its day. Labour has failed to recognise the need for greater opportunities and improved services for the Scottish people and to move with the times. The SNP interpreted the desire for change, and presented a convincing agenda of how to achieve it with many convincing policies. Within its membership, it has long been recognised that there are many people of different political colours from left, right and centre who will want to exercise these opinions when Scotland is independent. Their membership and allegiance for the SNP is because it is the only party with a dominating agenda for independence. When this is brought about – it is inevitable that these differentiating opinions will emerge.

Many people who voted for the SNP were not members of the party and if not members, were supporters of the other parties – Conservative, Lib/Dem. Greens and SSP. An in an independent parliament, there is likely to be keen competition from each political party for seats and high representation. This should result in a much healthier, virile and democratic society.

9 **Going independent would reward the anti-English sentiment that already exists in Scotland. The thousands of English people living in Scotland (and the Scots living in England) would be forced to move.**

This is becoming an outmoded question and might be interpreted as emotive scaremongering. Unfortunately there remains some antipathy towards the English and it manifests itself unpleasantly in some areas. However we are living at a time where this is a great increase in mobility particularly by younger members of our society and racial, disrespectful comments are disliked and are treated with contempt.

Are we suggesting here that an independent Scotland would behave in a manner that would force the English to move? This cannot be – even the slightest slight whiff of something that smacks of even a veiled suggestion of 'ethnic cleansing would be unthinkable and totally abhorrent to the great majority of Scots.

If Scotland adopted a stance where it resented incomers particularly the English, many of the fair-minded Scots and not the English would be amongst the first to leave.

Scots have integrated well in England for centuries, and their emphasis on good education, sense of family and thriftiness is respected. They also enjoy prominence in the news media and are noted as being good communicators.

(There is a sense that the present concentration of Scots in the Cabinet may be starting to ruffle a few feathers, but performance rather than race may well be the cause.)

As a Scottish government concentrates on improving education, social welfare and job prospects for all its citizens, even more opportunities and skills will be required. Already there is a marked increase in Scots returning to take up positions in Scotland again. There is a greater need for Scotland to welcome the talents that others bring. Insularity must be avoided at all costs.

10 **Within a few years, the Scottish electorate would revert to type and Scottish politics would be left/socialist/ Labour dominated for generations to the detriment of the Scottish economy – especially regarding inward investment.**

If Scotland reverted to type then it would be to the traditional open and internationalist perspective that characterised Scotland before the dull hand of the Union fostered defensiveness and negativity in some quarters.

11 **We'd need frontier posts all along the border.**

They do not need them between the EU countries that are members of the Schengen Agreement, there is no reason on earth why we would need them between Scotland and England. It would not be in interests of Scotland or England.

12 **We'd be forced to join the Euro.**

It would be our choice whether or not to join the Euro, a choice in which we only have a minority voice just now.

13 **If you and your family are living on subsistence income in Stornoway, whether the Government is in Edinburgh or London makes no difference.**

There is less chance of the Stornoway family living on subsistence income under independence because the government would at least know where Stornoway was, what the needs of its population were, and tailor policies to deal with these needs.